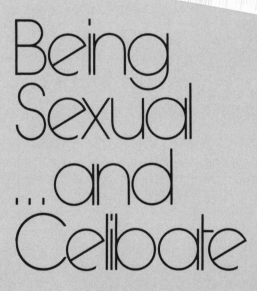

Being
Sexual
...and
Celibate

Other books by Keith Clark, Capuchin

MAKE SPACE MAKE SYMBOLS

AN EXPERIENCE OF CELIBACY

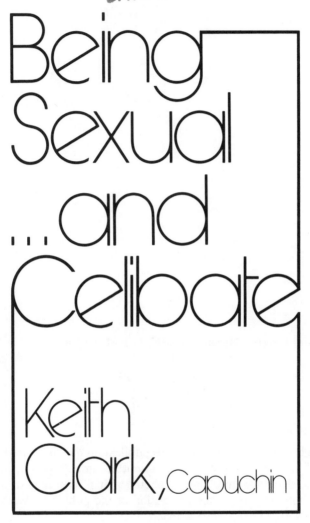

Being Sexual ...and Celibate

Keith Clark, Capuchin

AVE MARIA PRESS
Notre Dame, Indiana 46556

Imprimi Potest: Myron Kowalski, O.F.M. Capuchin
                  Provincial Minister
                  The Province of St. Joseph
                  Detroit, Michigan
                  August 22, 1985

Library of Congress Catalog Card Number: 85-73158

International Standard Book Number: 0-87793-328-6
                                    0-87793-329-4 (pbk.)

Printed and bound in the United States of America.

Contents

INTRODUCTION

Jerry and I had spent most of the evening speaking with one of our brothers in the Order about our views on human sexuality. Jerry had just finished articulating with great clarity a point he was making. Our brother said, "That's really good. Are you going to collaborate with Keith on his next book or are you only going to be mentioned in the foreword?"

"I'm going to be mentioned in the foreword," Jerry answered without hesitation. "He writes; I don't!" Have you ever found yourself the presenter of ideas which were so much the product of a joint effort of your teachers, colleagues and friends that your solo presentation distorted the truth and the impact of what you had to say? That is my position as I present the ideas in these pages. I have not conceived them in isolation; they are my reflections on what a great many people have shared with me of their own experience. I do not articulate the thoughts alone. It is in dialogue with Jerry, Jan, Ron and Paul that the ideas found words.

Those who have read *An Experience of Celibacy* (Ave Maria Press, 1982) have already met these friends of mine. When the manuscript for that book was ready for reworking into a final draft, I mentioned to Jerry that I was going to change his name in order to save him any embarrassment. He asked me not to do that. "I'd like you to use my name," he said, "because I'm glad if anyone can benefit from my experience." The responses of the others were similar.

This book is much more fully a collaborative effort of the five of us. Speaking plainly to each other about our experience has generated our reflections and eventually those reflections found articulation. Only with their encouragement did I begin and continue to write and rewrite what you are about to read.

This book, then, has a point of view. I have not arrived at the point of view alone, nor have I surveyed others to gather the data of their experience, nor have I collaborated in researching the topic of human sexuality. The point of view comes primarily from what I have experienced and has been clarified and refined in conversations with friends.

It has been tested against what I have heard from others as they spoke directly or obliquely of their experience— men and women, young and old, heterosexual and homosexual, married, single and celibate, priests, lay and religious. What they said made sense to me because I heard their stories from my point of view.

The old adage that "a little knowledge is a dangerous thing," I think, is especially true in matters of sexuality. Anything a person knows or thinks about sexuality, if it is unrelated to his or her *own seriously examined experience* of being sexual, falls into this category. Scientists can research the biological aspects of sexuality or speculate about the bio-psychological elements; philosophers and religionists can comment on the personal/spiritual level; and any darn fool can generalize about the interpersonal and social realities of being sexual. All of them, from professionals to darn fools, can shed light on the subject, but only for those who are in touch with what they know from experience.

I don't mean to imply that we must have experienced every aspect of sexuality before we can know something about the subject. I mean only that we need to be in touch with our own experience of being sexual before we accept what anyone else has to say about any aspect of being sexual.

Whatever understanding we arrive at will not serve us well unless we are in touch with what we know for sure from our own experience.

In *An Experience of Celibacy* I shared my observations and reflections and opinions in a rather narrative fashion. The many responses I received indicated that people found it helpful, largely because they were encouraged to admit to themselves that they had experiences similar to mine. What I found is that most of the discussion which the book generated had little to do with celibacy. Rather, they revolved around what I didn't write explicitly—my assumptions about human sexuality. This book is about my experience of being sexual and the philosophical and theological assumptions I have about what I've experienced.

I'd like to be as "down-to-earth" in my writing this book as people said I was in the previous one, but that is more difficult. This book is very much a spelling out of my philosophical and theological opinions. It is less my experience and more *the stories* I tell myself about what I have experienced. In this volume I invite you not only to be in touch with what you know for sure because you've experienced it, but to examine the stories you tell yourself about that experience, and to recognize where and from whom you've gotten those stories.

This is my viewpoint on sexuality. I do not mean to define what sexuality is; I mean only to describe the way I see what's there. I do not want to present my thoughts in an attempt to convince readers that being sexual and celibate must mean for them what it has come to mean for me. On the other hand, I do not want to pretend that my outlook is merely a tentative or speculative statement. I am convinced of what I write. I am convinced enough to think that many others may find what I have to say helpful in their own exploration of being sexual and celibate.

I do not want to present what I have written on these pages as the "last word" on the matter. It is not even the "last word" in my own understanding of what I have experienced and heard. I presume I will continue to speak with friends about what I experience, and from them hear quite a different experience. Together we will most likely continue to try to make sense out of what is obvious but mysterious about being sexual. I philosophize and theologize a bit in these pages. And as I typed them for the final draft I felt a bit uneasy. I think just about everyone I know can take exception to something I have said. And most of the people I know can feel supported in their opinions about sexuality by something else I have said in these pages.

I was at a lecture once, where a respected professional psychologist said, "As Clark says...," and proceeded to quote something I had written, doing so in support of a position he was expounding. I felt as though I had been kidnapped and dragged into the realm of the "experts." I was flattered to be quoted by someone I respect. But the words I had written sounded entirely too weighty in the context in which they were spoken.

What I write in these pages is my opinion about being sexual and celibate. Feel free to take it that way. It is not the opinion of a professional researcher, nor that of a philosopher or theologian. But, as Clark says, "All of them, from professionals to darn fools, can shed light on the subject, but only for *one who is in touch with what he or she knows for sure because he or she has experienced it.*"

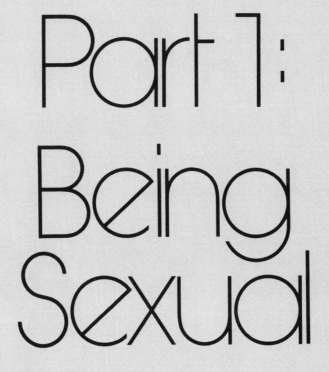

Part 7:
Being
Sexual

Chapter 1
And Then I Was Born

I don't remember what it was like in my mother's body. And I don't remember when I first became conscious enough even to know that I was anywhere, because my ability to reflect on my experience would not awaken in me for many years. But at some point in my development I could be physically and emotionally receptive to whatever my environment offered even in my mother's womb. And even in my mother's womb I could respond physically and emotionally to whatever stimulated me. It wasn't until I was born, though, that I could experience what my mother's womb had been for me.

I don't remember being born either. But physically and emotionally it was my first experience of separation from one to whom I had been joined. Prior to my birth, my environment had accommodated itself to my every need. My physical needs were complex, and meeting them required more ingenuity than my mother could have managed by even the most dedicated conscious and deliberate effort. But my mother's body had a wisdom of its own over which her conscious and deliberate choices had little control. And my own body had an unconscious wisdom which allowed me to receive what she provided.

My emotional needs were less complex before I was born. Simply being in an environment which touched and surrounded me in a friendly way was enough. I was wanted and cherished. Many years later my mother told me rather obliquely that my presence inside of her might have been a problem. Apparently she wasn't supposed to be able to bear any children, and her pregnancy worried those who loved her.

The emotional environment in which Mom lived while she was carrying me was ambivalent. She was excited that there was going to be a me, she told me 25 years later when her own health was failing. But there was concern about whether my growing inside her would be the end of her. But inside her womb, I experienced only that uncomplicated emotional environment of being connected to another human being. The storms outside didn't reach me.

I cannot recall on any of the events which preceded my birth, nor do I have any conscious memory of my first three and a half years. What I can now reflect on are the stories I have heard from Mom, Dad and others who remember me then. I can also reflect on the circumstances which surrounded those who remember me and my family.

Mom told me that she cried when she first saw me, because I was so small. "I like my men tall," she said. That's obvious from the fact that my father is over six feet tall.

My physical needs became somewhat less complex after my birth, and meeting them could be managed by the conscious, deliberate and dedicated efforts of my parents and the hospital staff and Doctor Baer who had delivered me. There was still an instinctual emotional wisdom in my parents and those who supported them which allowed them to respond to my emotional needs. Mom and Dad touched, held, fed and cherish me, they claimed me as their own. And the conventional wisdom of their environment, as well as those accepted as experts in the matter, told them to go right ahead and do so.

The physical intricacies of my life-support system were greatly reduced after I was pushed and pulled from that warm supportive place inside my mother. I no longer needed to be connected physically with another living human being. My body temperature could be kept constant by its own metabolism, and a sufficient supply of blankets could replace the womb. My own lungs and diaphragm and heart now brought oxygen to my brain and other organs. I was able to move more freely and by my own physical efforts I could seek out the nipple which was offered to provide nourishment. But my ability to provide for myself was severely limited. I could cry when I needed *something*, and usually Mom and Dad could figure out what it was I needed.

The complexities of meeting my emotional needs increased immensely at birth. I had been driven from a place of the most simple emotional union into an environment already beset by emotional storms which had not touched me. And my arrival in this place added turbulence to the atmosphere. My emotional needs were also turned over for gratification to the instincts and insights of those who tended me.

After my birth I was no more self-sufficient emotionally than I was physically, but I now could be left alone! For the first time in my life I could experience being separate, needy, incomplete, insufficient, and alone. From now on, any sense of connectedness with other human beings would depend on my ability to establish a relationship with them and on their ability and willingness to relate to me.

From the womb I carried with me the instinct to establish relationships with others. Being driven from the womb was itself the impetus to want to regain a sense of connectedness with others. Physically and emotionally my womb experience was imprinted forever on my psyche. I can't reflect on any personal memory of it. But I can reflect on what I remember of my experiences and behavior over the past 46 years and I can know that *something* happened to me before I can remember it, and that something has profoundly influenced most of my experience and behavior and has inclined me to seek connectedness with other human beings.

Much later in my life my conscious mind and my ability

to make choices awakened in me. I am aware of my craving to be connected with other human beings and I can hypothesize that the origin of this craving is in my conception and birth. I can theologize that my sense of incompleteness is put there by God who created humankind—"male and female He created them." But with my conscious mind and my free choice I seem able to do no more than manage the experience which is more primitive in me than my insight and freedom.

As my body was formed by the physical intricacies of my mother's womb, it was provided with a biological apparatus for genital sex. A dozen or more years of life outside my mother's womb would have to pass before this biological apparatus reached maturity, but I was separated from my mother's body only after I had been equipped physically with the possibility of again experiencing physical union with another human being.

Long before I became very aware of my physical sexual responses to mechanical and psychic stimuli, I began to behave in ways which brought a sense of emotional closeness to others. Family was very important to me. Dad had a large easy chair whose arms were worn thread-bare by our sitting on them as he read the newspaper. I had a sense that, although a bother to him in his attempt to learn of the day's events from *The Monroe Evening Times*, my presence was pleasant for him. Grandpa Bolender's lap was also a familiar perch as we blew on the cover of his golden pocket watch to make it magically open in his hand. And Grandpa Clark's knee was part of appropriated territory on which we felt welcomed; there we learned that the whittling knife must always move away from us, not toward us.

Mom listened! Although her listening seldom distracted her completely from the mix-master or from making beds or ironing, I sought out her company. Auntie Dell listened and taught. She seemed to use few words and was not affectionate in an effusive way, but she could be interrupted, I knew, whether she was at her game of solitaire or at the stove. And Aunt Edna allowed us into her huge house and read to us. Uncle Fred with his black-rimmed glasses seemed to be beyond my understanding, but he was definitely an occasional part of my childhood. Uncle George, Aunt Mag and Aunt Kate welcomed me into their home. And when I would give Uncle George the day-old newspaper from Grandpa Clark's he always found a coin or two to give me in exchange.

School was a frightening experience most of the time. But there too I made friends with the sisters and my classmates. John Riley became my closest friend. In about the fifth grade Tom Schaefer moved to town and we became lifelong friends.

By eighth grade some of my classmates who had not been friends became the objects of my curiosity and fascination. I think Peg Shea was the first girl I stared at. I didn't know why, but I did—from head to toe. Judy Hastrich and I fought; but it was different from the way I fought with Peter Wilson and occasionally with John Riley. But it was Jennifer Young who captivated me!

The same sort of process extended itself to adults and other kids in my life all during grade school. I got some concrete advice from my dad and mom once in awhile on how my relationship to one or another adult in my life might be improved. And somehow the circle of my relationships widened and my sense of being accepted and acceptable grew.

When I went to a high school seminary, there was a sudden break with the friends and classmates of grade school days. The closer relationships remained, but a whole new group of peers and adults abruptly entered my life. Two classmates and several teachers became lasting friends, but girls were banished from my relationships because they would draw me away from being a priest.

Women, however, remained friends. I kept contact with some of the Dominican Sisters who had taught me in grade school, and I got along best with the women in my job at the Monroe Clinic Pharmacy each summer. The summer after high school, since my family had moved away from Monroe, I got a job at Marshall Fields in Skokie, Illinois. The head of the boy's clothing department was Mrs. Franks. She liked me and I liked her. She hired me back the following summer even though I had been told at the employment office that there were no jobs available.

I joined the Capuchins after one year of college, and again I had a sense that I was breaking off relationships with friends and acquaintances, and even to some extent with my family. But I developed new friends and established new ties. I learned, as time went on, that even my conscious efforts and expectations of myself as a religious did not sever some of the relationships I had established growing up.

After seven years as a Capuchin I was ordained a priest and found myself entering into a new kind of conscious relationship with people. I was celebrating Eucharist and talking to people who wanted to "talk to a priest." A year later I was sent to New York for further studies and met a whole new group of peers. And with it, a whole new set of relationships. Two years later I was assigned to our novitiate where I spent seven years watching one class of novices after another walk through my life. With individuals in each class I established close relationships.

During those years at the novitiate I also fell in love for the first time in a deeply emotional way. During those years I was accepted first as a rather popular priest and then as a good friend by families in the area. Since I left the novitiate 10 years ago, I have travelled quite a bit giving retreats and workshops and I have established ties with men and women throughout this country and beyond its shores.

Since high school I have always had someone with whom I could share my experiences of sexuality, friendship, romantic feelings and relationships. In high school and during my seminary days there was always an older Capuchin with whom I felt free to reveal myself. Since ordination I've always had a trusted friend whose opinion I valued and with whom I could explore my experience of these central realities of my life. As I have entered into my middle years I have found myself more deliberately taking advantage of the opportunity to share deeply with those with whom I could have chosen to have merely a casual relationship. And my brothers and my father and new mother have an importance for me which invites from me increased efforts to spend time with them.

I regard *all* of these events, experiences and relationships as manifestations of my sexuality because they all had to do with establishing and maintaining a relatedness and connectedness to other human beings in varying degrees of personal intimacy.

As my emotional life developed and was given direction, another level of myself would awaken: The personal/spiritual level of insight and freedom. As a mature and maturing person I could with insight ascertain the meaning of my biological sexual apparatus and my emotional orientation toward other human beings. As a mature and maturing person I could freely choose the behavior which would direct my biological urges and emotional or bio-psychological drives toward a *personal* experience of what my body and my emotions remembered from the womb. I learned gradually that the connectedness which I crave can be experienced in personal intimacy with others.

I now regard my human sexuality as all those activities which stem from or lead to the gratification of my biological urges and emotional drives and which stem from and lead to the fulfillment of my personal need for intimacy. Those activities which stem from and lead to the fulfillment of my personal need for intimacy I regard as the specifically *human* aspects of my sexuality.

Sexuality is a much more pervasive reality in human life than most people I have spoken with seem to believe. Having taken considerable time to reflect rather seriously on our ex-

periences has led me and some close friends to suspect that
our sexuality is much more pervasive of our lives than we
first imagined. Dr. Sigmund Freud showed the pervasive nature of our sexual urges and drives. I am not thinking of
those biological and bio-psychological aspects of human sexuality when I tell myself that human sexuality is more pervasive than most people appreciate. I am referring to the pervasive influence of that in human sexuality which makes it
specifically human—our need for intimacy. The insistence of
this need for fulfillment and the havoc wreaked when it is
not met explains to me much of human interaction. It also
explains most of the frustration with life experienced so
deeply even by those who are "happily married" or "sincerely devoted" to the service of others through a celibate
lifestyle, by those who are dedicated to the single life, by
"swingers," by single parents who cope well, or by the wid-
owed who have adjusted to a new life. Much of the disappointment in the lives of celibate and married people, as
well as in the lives of all others, comes from failure to recognize the personal need for intimacy and from relying exclusively on the gratification of our biological sexual urges and
our emotional or bio-psychological sexual drives to bring
happiness into our lives.

A fuller understanding of our sexuality, one which recognizes our need for intimacy and helps us meet that need,
can bring a great deal of happiness to lives which otherwise
might be merely surfeited with pleasure or filled with disappointment.

Chapter 2
Our Levels of Sexuality

I'm not sure of their chronological order, but I know I've experienced three distinguishable levels of my own sexuality. I identify these as the biological, bio-psychological and personal/spiritual. I have experienced these in a very jumbled way, and not as tidily as my reflections on these experiences suggest. But the categories provide a way for me to think and talk about what I have experienced.

In the biological level I experience being sexual simply by having a biological sexual organ. I gradually came to understand more about how it works. It has to be stimulated mechanically but once stimulated its operation is directed by laws and instincts over which no understanding or lack of it seems to have any effect. In fact, I have understood and misunderstood my biological sexual make-up in a variety of ways since I reached puberty. I've wondered about it often. It was in eighth grade and freshman year of high school that I began to experience erections and wet dreams and the growth of hair in my armpits and around my penis; at that time my perspiration started to smell funny. My voice changed then too.

In high school we had a couple of formal classes on sexuality and I learned that I was not wetting the bed with urine! And with charts and diagrams and proper sexual terminology I heard and saw for the first time that this stuff called sperm came from my testicles and somehow got mixed with fluids from other glands.

I was as naive as anyone else in the room, but even the most naive among us knew that those who were telling us not to worry were in fact worried about telling us. So I worried about anything I thought might have anything to do with sex. If I had a wet dream, even though it was while I was asleep and therefore supposedly all right, I was sure it happened because I had been thinking about sexual things too much while I was awake. It was many years later that I was told that the erection and emission I experienced probably caused the dream and not vice versa.

It seemed as though I awoke each morning with an erection. Much later in life someone told me that an erection could be brought about by my sphincter muscle's soliciting some help in holding back the flow of urine from my full bladder.

There were a lot of other things I discovered about my biological sexual apparatus and how it worked as the years went on.

But the point is that there seemed to be an instinctive way in which my physical sexual apparatus operated and still operates. At puberty I simply became much more consciously aware of what had been there since birth. My exploration and understanding of my biological sexual level continues to grow.

As I got older and was educated in the ways and vocabulary of the people a generation younger than I—particularly by one class of novices after another—I could simply accept that some days I was physically "horny" and I could offer no explanation whatsoever. I blamed the phase of the moon and the season of the year until I had sufficient data to realize that it could happen to me any time of month in any season. At first the physical part of me seemed to have a life of its own. It almost seemed to be another person. Gradually I accepted my biological sexual level as simply part of who I am, and after that I no longer blamed "it" for doing all those troublesome things to "me."

I have come to think of my biological sexual level as that physical component of my sexuality which is instinctual and which once stimulated works according to its own wisdom. Girls who reach puberty, I used to think, got a lot more correct and accurate information than boys did. But I've heard from many women that they too were left pretty much to their own resources to figure out their experiences of their biological sexual level.

We should be familiar with our biological level, and we should understand the general pattern for the workings of our bodies, both in their physiological aspects and in the unique ways we experience our own body rhythms and cycles.

The impetus toward sexual activity of any kind which stems from my biological level I call biological sexual urges. They are instinctual in their urgency and in their operation. My biological level is the level of genital sexual pleasure. My limited experience and my not nearly so limited sexual fantasies assure me that at the biological level sex is fun because it's pleasurable.

I have also experienced an emotional or bio-psychological level of my sexuality. I have an orientation toward other human beings. Technically, this bio-psychological orientation has two prongs or aspects: there is my orientation in the gregarious sense—we come together with other human beings in groups—and in the mating sense. The gregarious inclination has some connection with sexuality, I think, but I don't experience it in the same way that I experience my inclination to come together with others in a mating sense. I think of the feeling of closeness I experience in casual friendships and the feelings which parents and children have for each other as part of the gregarious inclination of the bio-psychological level.

I was born with an instinct to relate to other human beings. I think of this instinctual orientation as an innate capacity which was developed by my family and my immediate society.

My first learning on the bio-psychological level of my sexuality was derived from simple biological fact that I was born with a penis.

This clearly observable physical reality triggered in those who attended me in infancy and childhood a whole set of expectations I was subtly induced to meet. Biologically I was male; that informed my parents that they should relate to me as male, and that in turn induced me to regard myself as a male and to develop very quickly a masculine gender identity.

My instinctual capacity to relate to other human beings finds its origin in my experience of connectedness with my mother before I was born and in the fright of separation I experienced at birth. My bio-psychological level is the emotional component of my sexuality and it was educated predominantly by the minute displays of emotion I got from people in my surroundings. I have no recollection about the emotional learning which took place. But I learned that some things were supposed to be sexually stimulating to my emotions and other things were not. Through this education, a set of rather mysterious receptors seems to have been put in place within my bio-psychological level and they pick up certain stimuli as sexually significant. I learned that kissing the girl next door was something to which I should respond sexually long before I could do so. I learned that undressing in the presence of anyone except my brothers was supposed to be sexually stimulating. At about the time I reached puberty I was introduced to strip poker, and sure enough, undressing in the presence of another was sexually stimulating!

Included among the receptors in my bio-psychological level is one which determines whether I respond sexually to members of my own sex or to members of the other sex. Experts debate whether this receptor is founded in biological factors or is totally learned or is a combination of both genetic and learned factors. However it happened, I learned unconsciously to respond differently to men and women. On my bio-psychological level, I also can respond to a particular person as "the right one." This is the conscious emotional component of my sexuality, the level of romantic interests and experiences and pursuits.

It's easy for me now to sort out my experience and to recognize where they fit in these levels. But at the time, all I had was the various experiences, all of them connected somehow with being sexual.

In some ways I regard my bio-psychological level as the connector between my biological level and the world outside myself. An actual person or situation is presented to me through my senses, or an image is concocted from memories of people and situations I have previously experienced as sexually stimulating, and my bio-psychological level initiates a sexual response in my biological level. This seems a terribly clinical way to talk about getting "turned on" in eighth grade by Peg Shea, but it is the way I think about that early adolescent romance.

I think about my bio-psychological level as having been educated from earliest childhood to respond to certain stimuli as sexual. Most often I was induced to accept as sexually significant those things which my elders considered sexually significant. The general orientation to the opposite sex or to our own sex is nuanced by the learning which goes on in one event after another in our childhood and youth. The result of that learning means that certain characteristics of other people's anatomy, activity and personality, as well as certain situations involving other people, will excite us in an emotional sexual way. I have a hunch that at certain periods of life anything which seems forbidden could become an object of sexual fascination if it has anything at all to do with our bodies. When we were young children and adolescents, sexuality was for many of us fascinating but forbidden.

What one culture considers sexual and induces its grow-

ing children to accept as such may differ greatly from what
is sexual in another culture. What is considered sexy by one
generation may be laughable in another. When I was in high
school we thought it was "sexy" to wear our hair slicked
back into a "ducktail"; we assumed the girls thought that
was sexy too. I doubt if women my age find anything very
sexy about men my age wearing their hair in "ducktails." I'm
pretty sure no high schooler today finds it very sexy.

There are names for some of our emotional sexual responses. If I find my own sex more fascinating than the other
sex, I am homosexual. If I prefer the opposite sex, I am heterosexual. And there are names for fetishes of all kinds. But
my own emotional sexual response is too individual to be totally captured by the names given to certain combinations of
sexual responses. No one quite knows what makes another
person "the right one" for him or her. I don't know either,
but I know when I meet that person.

I encourage familiarity with our own bio-psychological
levels. I think I should know what "turns me on." I'll probably never have it all figured out, but when I find myself responding emotionally to some "sexual object," I should be
aware of it. I know that the people to whom I respond emotionally change as time goes on, as does the response. Peg
Shea isn't sexually attractive to me the way she was in eighth
grade. For that matter had Peg and I married, she would be
sexually attractive in very few of the ways she was in our adolescence. I guess the learning which goes on in my bio-
psychological level continues throughout life.

The impetus toward sexual activity of any kind which
stems from my bio-psychological level I call bio-
psychological sexual drives. They are instinctual in their origin but learned through cultural education. At this level of
my sexuality I experience sex as exciting, even thrilling.

Much of the discussion of human sexuality seems to center around the biological and bio-psychological levels, and
comparisons are made between what humans experience

and what is true of the higher forms of animals. A lot of what I have heard and read relegates consideration of the personal/spiritual level to the domain of philosophers and theologians. The implication seems to be that anything said about sexuality beyond the biological and bio-psychological cannot be verified by empirical research, and has little value. Sociology claims to add to the discussion of human sexuality by researching human sexual behavior and the verifiable consequences of behavioral patterns in a given culture. Anthropology compares the sexual practices of various cultures. But human sexuality, like that of the higher forms of animal life, is thought by many to have been completely covered in its objective aspects when the biological and bio-psychological levels are studied.

I think I have experienced something sexual which is not merely biological or bio-psychological and which does not stem from the fact that I am a Christian and a Catholic. I am spiritual even if I have no interest in religion. I have experienced connecting with other human beings in ways which I cannot explain solely by my biological urges and bio-psychological drives.

Even the sexuality of the higher forms of animals is not totally explained by their biology and bio-psychology. There is something else operative in their sexual lives: the level of need. And the meaning of animal sexuality is determined by the need which is met by the animals' instinctively moderated sexual activity. Meeting the need is achieved, not through the having and the operation of the animal biology and bio-psychology, but by the instinctively moderated behavior.

In human sexuality there is also a third level of need which gives meaning to human sexual activity. But that need cannot be ascertained simply by observing human sexual behavior, because human sexual behavior, while instinctively motivated, is not *regulated* by instinct. It is regulated by the spiritual and personal capacities of insight and freedom.

With insight we human beings can see that the species needs more human beings. That need for the species to continue gives meaning to human sexuality.

But there is another human need which gives meaning to human sexuality. It is the need for intimacy with other human beings. It is the deepest personal need we have, and it is a spiritual need. We long to come together with other human beings so that our spirits touch and our personalities fuse without being lost in each other. In intimacy the expanse which separates us from every other human being is bridged, and the separateness, the insufficiency, the neediness which we inherit from our birth is temporarily alleviated.

The need for personal intimacy can also be recognized by insight. But insight does not mean humans will behave in ways which will insure the meeting of either the need for the species to be continued or the personal need for intimacy. We human beings are not instinctively directed in our activity. We must freely choose those behaviors which meet the needs we have recognized. The meaning of human sexuality is discovered only by insight and it must be pursued in freedom. Because my biological sexual urges and my bio-psychological sexual drives are not instinctively directed toward propagating the species or achieving intimacy, I can engage in biological and bio-psychological sexual activity for no purpose beyond the gratification of my urges and drives. These might be as much meaning as I can see in human sexuality, or it might be as much as I freely choose to pursue.

On the other hand, because my biological sexual urges and my bio-psychological sexual drives are not instinctively moderated, I can pretend even to myself that I don't experience them.

The meaning of human sexuality cannot be ascertained simply by observing human sexual behavior. Only the individual human mind aided by the collective wisdom of humanity can discover the meaning of human sexuality, because in humanity sexual behavior has been cut loose from the need which would insure that the behavior would have meaning.

Theologians and philosophers debate, sometimes heatedly, what that meaning is. I believe human sexual activity must meet a need for the species and for the individual persons if it is to have its fullest meaning. Sexual activity has meaning if the need of the species to be continued, and the need for the individual to connect personally is met. Otherwise sexual activity has no meaning beyond the gratification of sexual urges and drives.

Some people accept the gratification of urges and drives as sufficient meaning. I do not. Even animals are instinctively directed in their sexual activity to achieve more than that. My interpretation of what I have heard from married couples suggests that human sexual activity achieves its highest meaning when both the need for the species to be propagated and the need for intimacy are intended and pursued. Sexual activity which intends and pursues neither need ranks among humanity's most disappointing and devastating experiences.

I don't believe that married couples who love each other are supposed to enter into sexual activity encumbered with weighty thoughts and lofty ambitions! I presume sex is fun! It's a way for people who are permanently committed to each other to play, to enjoy each other, and to further their intimate relationship. Such play and fun has meaning, not because the partners' heads are full of ideas about "meaning" and "communication" and "self-disclosure," but because they have an intimate, committed relationship.

Sexual activity which is no more than the gratification of urges and drives is frequently portrayed as fun and fulfilling. But conversations I have had over the years with those who engaged in sexual activity in such a way have convinced me that genital sexual activity and romantic behavior of themselves will eventually disappoint, not because they are bad, but because they are not enough.

I have chosen a celibate life for myself, and my intent in my own sexuality does not include having a child of my own. I must find other ways to be generative. But my need for intimacy is as great as anyone else's. And intimacy is just as much a part of my sexuality as it is part of a married person's. Having decided not to marry and have children does not make my view of human sexuality that of an outsider.

"Human sexuality is about intimacy, period!" Jerry said one night. I told him I thought he had a point, but that he was overstating it. We argued and discussed the matter for several hours that night and on many other evenings. Eventually he convinced me. Human sexuality IS about intimacy. Not only about intimacy, but always about intimacy. Intimacy is possible for me because I was born a *sexual person*. Both words are important—"sexual" and "person."

Chapter 3
Intimacy Is Personal

Perhaps it was a particularly bad night for television. I suppose my disinterest in the programs triggered the critical melancholy with which I viewed the commercials interrupting the programs every 13 minutes. That night I found more annoying than usual the suggestion that intimacy could be brought into my life by wearing the right kind of jeans, splashing on the appropriate cologne, using the correct toothpaste and mouthwash, daubing on an expensive perfume, or even taking a laxative.

It was never directly asserted that the use of these items could introduce intimacy into my life, but I saw one anxious, isolated, harried person after another become surrounded by smiling appreciative faces after they performed the required activity with the appropriate product. Earlier in the evening I had noticed that hard-hats and country-western types are brought together best by drinking the right kind of beer. On my way to work the next morning billboards told me that brandy can do the same thing at campsites and cigarettes will do it at a cocktail party. Many products were advertised, but they all suggested the same thing—access to intimacy quickly.

The subtle and not so subtle pitch of many forms of advertising capitalizes on the pervasiveness of sexuality in human life. Doctor Freud discovered the sublimated presence of our urges and drives in many of our activities and desires.

Those urges and drives are given to us to lead us to achieve what we really need, namely intimacy.

The insight behind the pitch of those commercials and billboards is accurate. We all crave a connectedness with other people in romance, affection, camaraderie, shared enterprise. But the intimacy which will meet my need cannot be had so quickly by merely using a particular product. Even there in front of the TV set I could feel myself donning my imaginary shining armor and mounting my white stallion to venture out as the knight errant on a campaign to rescue a word from the ravages inflicted on it by the general usage of the population. The word I wanted to rescue this time was "intimacy."

On other occasions I have recognized the arrogance of my thinking that I have some right or duty to rescue a word from the variety of meanings and connotations it has. One March day on a beach in southern California I admitted to Paul that the reason I had brought along the notebook was my desire to think out some material for a workshop I was planning on sexuality. The particular segment I was working on was intimacy. That day I felt like championing the definition and descriptions of intimacy proposed by Erik Erikson. They were so satisfying to my mind and seemed so accurate in distinguishing intimacy from other human experiences with which it is often confused. "Intimacy is the fusing and the counterpointing of personalities," I said. "It is the ability to enter into concrete affiliations with others and the ethical strength to abide by those commitments," I insisted.

Paul said, "Let's try to articulate concretely what intimacy is as we have actually experienced it." He spoke slowly and thoughtfully as though he were recalling words which he had previously committed to memory. In fact, he was putting into words for the first time what his own experience had taught him.

"I know a moment of intimacy has been reached when I am no longer preoccupied by concern about the other person's judgment or critique of what I share. Ironically, a moment of intimacy occurs when I have been with a person long enough to discover that there are differences between us.

"In intimacy I never want to harm, manipulate or try to convince someone of anything beyond what I believe is good for that person.

"Intimacy is possible only after you have known a person long enough that you can affirm him or her concretely, because of your appreciation of that person's gifts. The affirmed knows that for the time being the one who is affirming regards him or her as the most important person there is. But there is the assumption that after this moment both will carry on independently.

"In this moment of time no other preoccupation or person is as important as you and your well-being. There is an unself-conscious realization that after this time other people and other concerns will preoccupy both of us. And that realization contributes to the giving process. A moment of intimacy occurs when the goal of life's deepest pursuit is surprisingly met; but having reached that goal, the moment remains intimate only with the willingness on the part of each to surrender what has been achieved."

I still believe in what Erikson defined, but my own experience of intimacy finds expression in what Paul articulated.

Being together on that beach with a friend and knowing it would be a long time before I'd see him again was a moment of intimacy. Neither of us felt the need to make something special happen that afternoon. We were simply enjoying each other's presence, some sun, sand, surf and conversation. We did not hide our concerns from each other; neither did we intrude into each other's private thoughts and feelings. Paul is my friend. He has allowed me to know him over a good many years. And he understands me, at times even when I can't understand myself. The intimacy we experienced found expression in neither genital sex nor in romantic activity.

I have intimate relationships with other people. The particular way I experience that intimacy is different with each person, but what Paul said in describing his own experience fits all those relationships in my life which I consider intimate.

Intimacy is so bound up with notions of romance and genital sex that I sometimes hesitate to describe the relationships I have or a time like I had with Paul as intimate. I experience a great deal of intimacy with Ron and Jerry and Paul and Jan, and with each of them I have spent more than one "intimate evening." If I am asked how my time with Jan was, I'll probably say truthfully that it was fun, nice, pleasant, enjoyable, worthwhile or just plain good. But to me the most important thing about the time I spend with her—as well as that I spend with Ron and Jerry and Paul and a good many other men and women—is that it is intimate. I allow them to know me and they allow me to know them.

In the presence of those with whom I have an intimate relationship, I feel invited to *be* myself and to *reveal* myself. I have a sense that they feel the same with me. When we can be ourselves and reveal ourselves to each other, something grows between us.

Intimacy has never happened for me instantly. I have been instantly attracted to some people the first time I laid eyes on them. Sometimes that attraction is sexual and sometimes it isn't. The attraction I have felt for others at times has led me to speak to them. On rare occasions, that has led quickly to our feeling safe enough to be ourselves and reveal ourselves without great hesitance. In doing so, an intimate relationship has begun, needing only to be nourished by the continued non-manipulative disclosure of ourselves to each other.

Fascination with another person happens to me instantly sometimes. That person possesses those qualities of body or personality which stimulate the receptors in my bio-psychological level. I am inclined to stare at that person exactly the way I stared at Peg Shea in eighth grade. I really don't know why I find some people fascinating, but I do. I know I am fascinated when I return home and announce that I have just fallen in love or have just met my best friend.

I remember returning home one evening from a meal with two friends at a restaurant featuring a Hawaiian Luau. I went to my room to do my customary writing, intending to pray after I had gotten in touch with and sorted out the day's events. All I wrote about was Natalie, one of the dancers in the Polynesian show.

I described every detail of her physical appearance, the interaction between us as she invited me to take part in the Hula instruction and as I declined the invitation. I went on to describe what I presumed of her personality and attitude. I was simply captivated and fascinated by Natalie!

That was fascination, not intimacy. Natalie stimulated a whole lot of the receptors in my bio-psychological level! I had to presume all kinds of things about her personality because I knew so little about her. Because of what I had experienced and found pleasing, I could construct in my imagination the ideal woman I wanted her to be.

Had I no previous commitment and therefore been free to pursue my initial fascination through seeing her more often it's possible that the initial fascination could have developed into a full-blown infatuation. And the infatuation could have led to romantic pursuits and behavior.

For me, romantic pursuits are those activities which stimulate our sexual emotions for another and are designed—consciously or unconsciously—to evoke a similar emotional response from another. Although romance can distort our perception of one another, it can also lead us to a sense of safety and relatedness with one another which will allow us to eventually be ourselves and reveal ourselves to one another. If we do, intimacy can arise from the romantic

pursuits. Romance is not intimacy, but it can lead us to behave in ways which will allow intimacy to arise. What is important is that we recognize with our insight and pursue
with our free choice those behaviors which will bring us together without anyone being dominated, manipulated, mu-
tilated or changed.

A good friend, a perpetually professed woman religious
for about ten years, told me very matter-of-factly one evening that she was quite sure that she would be seeking a dis-
pensation from her religious vows. I was shocked. In fact, I
said to her, "You're kidding!" and took another bite of the
Chinese food we were sharing. Then I looked at her expression, set my fork on the plate, and said to myself more than
to her, "No, you're not kidding."

She told me of a man who had been instantly able to
invite her out of herself like no one else had ever been able to
do. She was both popular and respected within her community, a potential leader because she was intelligent, witty,
personable and sympathetic. As the evening together continued, she told me of her own sense of isolation within her
community. She was becoming very aware of her great need
for intimacy, for connectedness. Randy entered her life and
invited from her a response no other person had ever invited;
and she responded. She found she could be open with him—
completely open. "He loves all of me," she said with feeling
too great and too real to be dismissed.

Within three months she had taken a leave of absence
from her community and had moved in with Randy. During
the course of those three months we spoke several times, and
she appeared to me to be completely infatuated with Randy.
Over those months she had told several of her sisters in the
community of her decision, and saw the pain and sadness in
each of their faces. But she regarded leaving as something
she had to do. Being with Randy had awakened in her feelings and responses which she had never had before. She attributed to Randy the ability to make her feel what she felt.

And she therefore attributed to him the response she gave him. "He makes me feel so free, so loveable, so able to be myself."

She cried with almost every one of her sisters whom she told about her decision to leave. At first, with real pain and disappointment and eventually with some deep anger, she asked why it was only when she was leaving that her sisters seemed to reach out to her. "Now that it's too late they are willing to get close," she said to herself in my hearing.

I tried arguing with the stories she told herself. But I lost every argument. I remain convinced that she found Randy "the right one," the one who stimulated her romantic sexual emotions and she became fascinated and then infatuated with him. These emotions led her to behave in ways which allowed intimacy to begin to arise in her life. She told her sisters one by one, and the revelation of herself to them and their response gave her the first taste of intimacy she had experienced with them. And she resented them for being too late.

By the time she left, she was in fact experiencing intimacy with a lot of people. She chose behaviors with Randy which were romantic as well as intimate; romance had awakened in her the inclination for behaviors which allowed intimacy to arise. Intimacy had come into her life on the wings of romance, and she really couldn't imagine that she could experience intimacy without romance.

Randy is a Catholic who was free to marry my friend. My friend said he loved all of her. But he didn't love her commitment to a way of life which precluded her marrying him. In their coming together a very significant part of my friend was obliterated. That having taken place, I imagine that their life together will be as happy as any other life. I assume that genuine intimacy will continue to grow between them. I don't know what happens to the realization in my friend that part of her is gone. She chose to have it be gone; I can't argue with her for that. But she did so by telling herself the story: "He loves all of me." I do argue with that.

The stories I tell myself about romance and intimacy come from my experience of being in love. I too have been loved by a woman who felt as romantically inclined toward me as I did toward her. I too told my brothers in the Order of my feelings for her. And they marvelled, feared, laughed and cried with me. I too thought seriously about romantically pursuing this woman. I didn't think at first of marrying her, just behaving toward her in ways which would continue the stimulation of my romantic feelings and perhaps encourage her romantic feelings for me. Ten years later she is still the woman I would want to marry. Her romantic feelings for me were never acted out. I never received from her any "mixed messages" which suggested that she wanted me to leave the Order and marry her. Nor did I give her any such messages. Today we talk about our relationship over the years, and she says to those who occasionally ask her why she never married me, "I love him too much to try to take him away from his commitment." She loves all of me. The intimacy we share is as great as any I have experienced in my life. It is an intimacy arrived at without romantic activity. Her love is one of the greatest gifts of my life.

At birth my personality was like a tiny seed. What there was of it could come together with other personalities, particularly those who nurtured and parented me, without either being lost in the other. Through my connectedness to them my own personality develops. Later in my infancy and early childhood I went to some lengths to demonstrate that I was mine even though I was theirs. Emotionally I didn't want to sever the relationships which were there, but I willfully insisted on indulging the impulses of my own body and then willfully insisted on *not* indulging them when Mom and Dad wanted me to. Much of my training and upbringing could be accomplished only because I had the need to be accepted by those who count and a need to be myself. My need to be accepted induced me to choose those patterns of acting which eventually coalesced into the personality which is mine. My need to be connected with others was a tool used in forging the person I have become.

These two needs which all through life can seem so contradictory were revisited when I was a teen-ager, right at the time when we experience what we call an identity crisis. I needed to be uniquely me, but I also had to know that I belonged. All during later adolescence and even into young adulthood, one of these contradictory impulses—to be me or to belong—could be indulged with such passion as to seem to exclude the other.

During this time adolescents try out the variety of possible concrete affiliations which are open to them. As the sense of self stabilizes, the willingness to belong increases. I-love-you/I-hate-you relationships, off-again/on-again marriages and in-again/out-again seminary and religious life experiences appear clearly to be externalized renditions of this inner conflict.

During this time of transition the individual consolidates the gains of childhood into patterns which seem to promise a successful adulthood. A life commitment usually signals the establishment of an identity. A surrendering of that commitment can take place only with the consequent tampering with who we are. Any such surrender of an essential part of our identity in order to come together with another is not intimacy.

In childhood the connectedness, the nurturance, the affirmation and the domination by parenting, disciplining and teaching adults are designed to induce the growing child to become somebody.

In adulthood the person still needs nurturance and affirmation and connectedness. But adults do not grow because of direct or covert attempts by others to dominate them. Being induced to change some part of our personality or being manipulated into changing a life commitment which has helped solidify our identity does not add to our growth as a person. It stunts it.

Adulthood is characterized by an ability to entrust ourselves freely to concrete affiliations with others without the fear of losing ourselves. Those of us who have not established an identity may also come together with others, but we are liable to do so in order to establish our own personal identity at the expense of the others. The assumption about adults is that the seminal personality which first engaged others during infancy has grown to a point in its own identity that it no longer needs to feed on other personalities. The assumption about mature and maturing adults is this: they are sustained by intimate relationships. We do not nurture and sustain ourselves at the expense of the other; we do not try to induce the other *to become* somebody. What is gained by each adult in a relationship is drawn from the relationship; what is felt for the other person is gratitude and appreciation, not indebtedness.

What does all this have to do with sexuality? My inclinations to connect with other human beings are part of my experience of being sexual. Whether it is because of biological urges, bio-psychological drives or my personal need for intimacy.

Intimacy is always personal. It can be expressed in genital activity; it can be expressed in romantic activity.

Genital sex and romantic activity can take place without intimacy. And, as I experienced with Paul on a beach in southern California, intimacy can be experienced and expressed without genital or romantic behavior.

Whenever we disclose ourselves in the hearing of another, intimacy is allowed to arise. The experience or the behavior of any one of us merely makes more apparent what is essentially true of each of us. No matter what you disclose about yourself in my hearing, my hearing of your disclosure will increase my own self-awareness. If I in turn disclose to you my increased self-awareness, and you hear what I tell you, your self-awareness will increase. Intimacy is the fusing and the counterpointing of personalities.

Everyone needs intimacy. Everyone craves it.

But intimacy is not found; it doesn't just happen. It can arise unexpectedly for those of us who are sufficiently in possession of ourselves to disclose who we are in our dealings with others. Our disclosure may put others in touch with themselves and evoke from them a similar disclosure. The dynamics by which interpersonal intimacy is allowed to arise are self-awareness and self-disclosure in the hearing of another.

I don't mean to imply that intimacy and the dynamics which allow it to arise must involve a lot of talking. I'm sure my tears shared with a friend at our parting, and my laughter at what we both find incongruous in ourselves, my embrace at our meeting, my touch and my just sitting silently have disclosed more about me than my words have. Speaking is just one of the behaviors I can choose in order to disclose myself.

When I allow others to see me and to experience the way I live I am disclosing myself, sometimes more accurately and clearly than I do if I try to explain myself.

I don't think about intimacy in particularly rigid categories. But in some more informal sort of way, I think that the level of intimacy which is possible depends on the level of disclosure which is employed. To the extent that I remain a mystery even to those with whom I am most closely associated, intimacy is not present between us. The kind of intimate relationship which is established by the self-awareness and self-disclosure in the hearing of another will be determined by the behavior by which the intimacy is expressed.

I distinguish for myself five levels of self-disclosure. The lowest of these is the communication of data about myself. I can tell a person that I was born on February 13, 1939, in Monroe, Wisconsin, and that person knows something about me.

Reporting such data can begin a process of self-disclosure which can allow intimacy to arise. Once in a lecture I mentioned that I had been a novice master and a man in the group who was currently a novice master came up after the lecture and introduced himself. We talked for several hours that evening, and we have kept in touch.

After *An Experience of Celibacy* was published, I received a great many more letters than I could have expected. The majority of them began, "Dear Keith, I hope you don't mind my calling you by your first name. After reading your book, I feel as though I know you." A lot of the letters went on to tell me that my speaking of my own experience had encouraged the reader to examine his or her experience. It was my self-disclosure which prompted an increase of self-awareness for others. It wasn't only that they knew more about me; it was the fact that I had *told them* which seemed to bring us together.

I think of the next level of self-disclosure as my expression of my opinion—what I think about something or someone. It's the stories I tell myself about what I know for sure from my experience. If I tell a friend that I think Monroe, Wisconsin, is one of the finest and most economically stable small towns in the state, he might not know any more about Monroe and he might disagree with my opinion, but he could know more about *me*. He would know my opinion about something.

As anyone who knows me already realizes, I like to think about what I experience and about what others tell me. I often talk about what I have come to think about my experience. There are some with whom I disclose my opinions about sexuality, for instance, and sharing those opinions has been a basis of the friendship which has developed. Jan and Jerry and I give workshops on sexuality and celibacy. We spend a lot of time sorting out our thoughts in our attempts to respond to the questions we are asked. Our friendship is based on more than our shared opinions, but they know me at that level better than most people do, and that is part of the intimacy we experience.

The next level of self-disclosure is my expression of feelings. If I tell someone how I feel about them or about someone else, they know a lot more about me. Again, someone could surmise that I have certain feelings about people and things, but when I tell that person my feelings, I disclose something very significant about myself: I reveal what something means to me.

I tell you what I think about you when I say, "You're very kind." But if I tell you, "I like you and I appreciate what you've done," I tell you more about myself and what you and your actions mean to me. You can be inclined to argue my opinion about you, because you disagree with it. Maybe you don't think you are all that kind. But you cannot argue about my feelings toward you. What can you say if I tell you I like you? "No, you don't"?

A still higher level of self-disclosure is the level of attitudes. Attitudes are decisions I have made about the way life is or the way it ought to be. They are similar to opinions in that they are stories I tell myself. But they differ from opinions in that attitudes are more generalized stories about life. The decisions I have made about how life is or how it ought to be are not merely cognitive; they are also emotional. In a sense an attitude is the combination of opinion and feeling. But the feeling, like the opinion, has been generalized; it is now an emotional response to a category of people, events or things, not merely to an individual person or event or thing.

I am liable to reveal my attitudes in ways other than directly reporting them. For instance, if I have an attitude that life is gracious, I will reveal that most often by the number of times I express gratitude for what someone else has done for me or appreciation for what I have seen another person do for someone else. If I have an attitude of superiority, I will reveal it most often by complaining and criticizing the behavior of others. Or it is also possible that if I have an attitude of inferiority I may reveal that attitude by trying "to bring everyone else down to my level" by my criticizing and complaining. Chances are others may recognize my attitudes before I do.

Prejudices are attitudes. I can change the cognitive aspect of my attitudes more easily than I can change the emotional component. If I was mistreated by a lawyer, for instance, I can rationally tell myself that all lawyers are not like the one I met, but I have an emotional memory which is not touched by the cognitive information. I may spend my whole life tensing up at the sight of a glass in a door which lists the law partners.

The highest level of self-disclosure is the level of faith. It is the most difficult level to communicate directly, because almost all attempts to communicate what I believe is couched in the language of theology, and is expressed, therefore, as an opinion. If I tell you what I pray for in regard to myself, you might get a glimpse of my faith: "I ask God to heal me of my cynicism." Or if you could hear me talking to God, you might get a glimpse of what I believe. Faith is the sense that I know I am known by the Other, not because God is all-knowing, but because I have made myself known. It is much more difficult to disclose my faith to another than is commonly believed. But if I manage to disclose that to you, you know me at a very deep level.

Frequently a person's faith is most readily disclosed by allowing one's praying to become transparent to another, even in public worship. It is disclosed, however obliquely, in the unself-conscious gestures, facial expressions, tears and devotion one exhibits.

The kind of intimate relationship I achieve with another person depends on the kind of expression I give my self-disclosure. I can communicate to another through romantic activity that I love that person. By that romantic self-disclosure I could establish a romantically intimate relationship.

If we communicate our affection for each other through genital sex without being manipulative or destructive, we experience a genitally intimate relationship. Intimacy can be experienced in friendship; it can be experienced in shared enterprise. It can be experienced in religious community life. The level of intimacy depends on the level of mutual self-disclosure; the kind of intimate relationship we establish depends on the expression which we give to our self-disclosure.

Intimacy doesn't happen instantly for me; it grows gradually, and frequently it begins because I find someone attractive enough to begin the process of self-disclosure. It can begin because we have something in common, or because circumstances have brought us together for purely functional reasons.

One afternoon Jerry came to my office to tell me that the night before he had finished writing a short story which he had been working on for several days. He had in his hand the typed pages, but he didn't give them to me to read; he began to read the story of Mandy, a young girl who leaves her home in search of those who told the story of the great king who refused to be one.

As he read to me, his feeling level increased greatly, and he revealed to me some deep feelings, some attitudes he had firmly espoused, and even some of his faith. The disclosure put me in touch with some of the things I had experienced in dealing with my own limitations and successes in my life. It was an intimate moment for both of us. He allowed me to know him by reading the story to me; his story put me in touch with some of my own experiences, feelings, attitudes and faith. I shared those with him.

It was a deeply intimate moment of friendship, reminiscent of a day on a beach in southern California when a friend had first put into words the elements which characterized for both of us what intimacy is like. I draw life from both relationships; and I am grateful, not indebted, to both of my friends.

Chapter 4
To Be Human Is to Be Lonely Sometimes

Some days I don't feel very appreciated. Experiences of friendship seem like memories so old that they just possibly are only creations of my need-driven imagination.

Those days can occur when I'm just about anywhere and without any apparent connection to what I am doing or to the people I am with. I usually don't immediately recognize that I'm feeling unappreciated or disconnected from those with whom I have previously experienced a moment of intimacy. Rather, I'm annoyed at the typewriter which isn't cooperating as well as it has on other days, or I catch myself making my third afternoon trip downstairs to get coffee for the office staff and it isn't yet three o'clock! No one in our office likes coffee that much! Instead of dealing with the business on my desk I find myself gravitating toward some person or group to whom I really have nothing to say and who are too busy with their own work to do any more than politely acknowledge my presence. At home the patterns are similar to those at the office. I sit in my room, writing or praying, while deliberately leaving the door open a crack so that someone might see my light on and "interrupt" me.

If I try to explain these kinds of behaviors, I tell myself stories about how outmoded my typewriter is and how I should have a word-processor; how non-consequential my work really is in any larger scheme of things; how lacking in concern is the general population of my world; or how willing I am to be available to anyone who might want or need to talk. I may even tell myself something about my health. It's easier for me to say to myself that I'm listless or bored or distracted or tired or coming down with something than it is to admit that I'm starting to feel lonely.

I have felt lonely often over the past 40 years. But only in the last dozen years have I admitted it to myself. Lonely is just something I thought I should not be unless a friend had recently moved away or died or I was away from home and familiar surroundings.

There's something scary about being lonely. It's a little like looking down Grandma Clark's cistern when we were kids. We were repeatedly warned not to go near that cistern and never—but never!—to walk on the wooden platform which covered it. When Grandpa took off the cover to fix it and to paint it grey-blue, we had to stand way back. We got the impression that even peering into it could draw us down to the bottom where we just knew we would drown. So we stayed away. We played on the back porch and were taught to admire the flowers which grew around the grey-blue platform; we hoped the butterflies we chased with our nets didn't go into those flowers, and we generally avoided all contact with that forbidden and dangerous part of Grandpa and Grandma's otherwise friendly back yard.

That's the way I feel about loneliness sometimes. I don't think about it that way, but that old cistern feeling comes back at moments when I'm aggravated by a non-cooperative typewriter or wandering around the office with a tray of coffee cups, or sitting in my room with my door ajar just a crack in the hope that my solitude will be interrupted.

Loneliness is on me at those times. But I keep the cover on it in good repair. I don't play around it. I pretend it isn't even there. I wouldn't think of uncovering it to peer inside; I might tumble in and never be heard from again. I might not be able to get out and maybe no one would be around to rescue me.

Most other people are as afraid of my loneliness as I am. Quite a long time ago I decided to give an honest answer to the often casual question: "How are you?" "Fine; how are you?" is not the only possible response to that question. "I'm giddy today," or "I'm preoccupied," or even "I'm sort of depressed," and "I'm angry," can be a startling response. But "I'm lonely," seems to be the response most difficult to deal with. It seems to evoke sympathy, concern, worry, guilt—"Maybe I should have done something for you earlier so you wouldn't feel that way!"—and a determination to directly or subversively alter my state of being lonely. The message is clear: "You shouldn't feel that way." And I can almost hear Grandma Clark asking me if I've been playing around the cistern again.

I used to be quite pleased with my repertoire of ways to ignore or deny that I felt lonely. I try not to do that any more, because I've come to believe that loneliness is not a problem, whereas attempts to avoid experiencing and looking at it have caused me some real problems.

I've reflected long and often on my own lonely moments and have arrived at a certain confidence in theorizing and generalizing about the experience.

My basic conclusion is that loneliness is a privileged experience because it prepares us for intimacy. How my musings have produced this conclusion is rather intricate.

Loneliness is a reality of our lives. I have listened to many men and women—married, single and religious—speak of their experiences of being lonely. But most of them don't identify what is happening as an experience of loneliness. I feel bad about that, because not being able to name what we experience makes it all the more confusing and frightening.

The framework from which I now view my own experience has been helpful to me and to several people with whom I've shared it. It helps me recognize and name what I'm experiencing. Familiarity with the dynamics of loneliness has helped me recognize the options for dealing with this rather pervasive reality.

The initial stirrings of loneliness take many shapes but they seem to have in common a vague dissatisfaction with who I am or with something about my current situation. I hardly ever recognize initially that what is happening is a simple moment of loneliness. I can, for instance, become dissatisfied with being alone even when it is by my own design. Or it can be for me a dissatisfaction with my participation in a group. The common element seems for me to be a dissatisfaction with my situation because I'm not connecting or connected with others in the way I want to be.

At times I can readily explain my disconnected feeling by the failures in communication between me and others; I just don't seem to grasp what is apparent to the others or I can't make myself understood. Sometimes I can explain my disconnected feeling by the unpleasantness of my environment: "I should have attacked the work on my desk before the piles of letters and papers and messages got so large." Sometimes it seems to be the routine or the stress of my occupation which induces my disconnected feeling. Sometimes it can be explained by the simple fact that I am alone and I no longer want to be alone. I have also experienced a general disconnectedness from life itself brought about by my fatigue. At other times I simply can't explain it. That's when the old cistern feeling returns most strongly.

But my initial dissatisfaction requests at least this of me, that I acknowledge it is there. I usually feel invited to search for an explanation which may be readily at hand. Whether or not I find a plausible explanation, my acknowledgment of the initial glimpse allows me to make decisions about how I will respond to the inner loneliness I am feeling.

If I simply reimmerse myself in the project which has brought me to be alone or reinvest my energies in the interaction of the group with whom I find myself, *without admitting* that I am feeling lonely, I am avoiding the experience of my own separateness, incompleteness and neediness. I may pretend to myself and to others that the worthwhileness of my projects or the depth of my relatedness to my group or the esteem in which I am held by many precludes the possibility that I should feel disconnected and dissatisfied. Acknowledgment of my lonely feeling would allow me to choose from a variety of options what I want to do with my experience of loneliness; ignoring or denying my lonely feeling, I have found, will lead me only into isolation from others. Having chosen to become aware of my sense of disconnectedness, I can work all the harder to be attractive or popular or involved or appreciated as a significant contributor to whatever I consider worthwhile projects and causes. But my sense of disconnectedness remains unacknowledged within me and can grow until I feel I am the *only* person who is adequately contributing to what is worthwhile. "I don't want to think of others as inferior to myself," I tell myself, "but the simple fact is that they are not as dedicated and involved as I am." And I will deal with them all condescendingly. Some few I will momentarily place on pedestals—those whom I meet and who seem to be more involved and dedicated and more popular than I. And I will be isolated from them because they are above me. I put them on a pedestal only momentarily, though; soon enough I will recognize their flaws and then I can minimize their contributions too. When I find myself speaking down to others or disparagingly of them, I now take it as a clue that I am feeling isolated from almost everyone because I have for too long a time ignored or denied my own sense of aloneness, separateness, incompleteness and neediness.

My initial glimpse of my disconnectedness doesn't lead to isolation; nor does reinvesting my energies in what I consider worthwhile or in interaction with colleagues. It's avoiding the acknowledgment of disconnectedness that eventually leads to isolation. My failure to accept myself as a separate, incomplete and needy human being isolates me from the others who are just like me. In effect, I refuse to admit that I am just like them!

If, however, I admit my initial glimpse I can decide what to do with this cistern-like experience. I may not want to explore its depths right now. There are other options open to me. I have decided occasionally simply to distract myself by listening to Beethoven's Fifth Symphony, which always engages me at the feeling level. By the final movement even my body is engaged in conducting the orchestra! At other times I have joined others in conversation or card games, or wrote to or called friends. What's important for me is to admit I'm feeling lonely and deliberately distract myself from my loneliness or do something to alleviate it, rather than simply avoiding it and pretending it isn't there. It helps me further if I can acknowledge to my friends that the reason I'm interrupting or writing or phoning is precisely that I'm lonely right now. I know that eventually I'll face my loneliness squarely and remove the grey-blue cover I have kept intact and explore that which is essentially true of me.

I consider all this the surface experience of loneliness. I am bound to feel lonely in this way simply because I was forced and invited from my mother's womb, an essentially alone, separate, incomplete and needy person. For 30 or more years I didn't recognize and name these surface experiences of loneliness as such, and I blamed a lot of people and circumstances for what I felt. I focused my attention on those other people and circumstances and could not choose any appropriate distractions or antidotes. I could only wish to change my surroundings, my occupation or even my way of life. And I felt isolated from others because I was divorced from my own experience.

Before I could enter into a deeper level of the experience of loneliness some significant maturing had to take place. As an infant I was needy in an almost total way. The roots of what I now know as loneliness were already in me. But as an infant I had no reflective sense that I needed anyone. Part of the care I required was to be protected from my own omnipotent behavior. I could recognize no need, no danger, no limitation on myself, and so I could neglect what I needed and reach out for what could injure me. I had no sense that a flame or shiny knife could harm me, no recognition that my arms and legs could safely carry me only as far as the edge of the bed or the stairway. My total neediness and dependence on others was accompanied by a total lack of recognition that I needed others. Getting fed was the only cooperative venture I entered into.

As consciousness grew I became aware of my need for and my dependence on others. I learned to assert my autonomy at times, but I couldn't deny my need for others.

In later childhood and early adolescence I became reflectively conscious of the interplay between my need for others and my desire for independence. I could deny at times that I had any need for anyone. But plans to run away from home always ended as fantasies, because I couldn't realistically get far enough away on my own to make the trip worthwhile.

During high school, I worked at the Monroe Clinic and got a real paycheck every week. With this first employment I was tempted to deny my need for others and to reflectively espouse emotional and physical self-sufficiency. It must have seemed ludicrous and annoying for the adults I was dependent on, but as a teen-ager I could, along with my peers, think of myself as independent and act that way.

My urge for independence and the recognition of the need I had for others played against each other when I was an older adolescent and the conflict was manifested outwardly in the many swings of emotion from totally dependent states to outrageous displays of autonomy.

After one year of college I joined the Capuchin Order and attained significant independence from my family, only to transfer dependence to my peers and elders in the Order.

As I look back I realize that my growing willingness to

admit I needed others was among the indications I was entering adulthood. I could resolve the conflict between my
desire to be independent and my need for others by reflectively espousing *interdependence*. During my early years in
the Order I was deciding on interdependence as an acceptable stance in life. At that point a mature and reflective experience of loneliness became possible for me at a level far
deeper than the surface level of physical and emotional disconnectedness.

The memory of a poster on a college dorm room wall
remains vivid 15 years later. It was a drawing of a naked
man seated on the ground, his head resting on his arms
which were folded and resting on his raised knees. The cap-
tion read: "The only cure for loneliness is solitude."

I still don't like the suggestion that loneliness is something to be cured like a disease or a problem. But I appreciate the suggestion that the most beneficial way to deal with
that initial glimpse I get of my aloneness, separateness, incompleteness and neediness is to enter deeply into it in a reflective solitude.

Such reflection is possible only when we have outgrown
childhood's total dependence on the nurturing of those
bound to care for us; and when we have laid aside the adolescent ploy of total independence.

Having accepted interdependence as a mature way of
life, we are still susceptible to the untrammelled activity of
our need for connectedness and are vulnerable to disappointment in our relationships. The need for connectedness remains. But the connectedness of interdependence must be
achieved and maintained. Only those persons confident of
their identity can establish and maintain the connectedness
of intimacy with others. The experience of the disconnectedness of loneliness remains too. And it too can be entered into
at a new depth.

My first experience of entering more deeply into a

lonely moment was unintentional. It is still vivid for me and succeeding entries into life's lonely moments have been confirming of what happened that day I sat daydreaming. But no subsequent event is as vivid.

I was sitting in my office facing the not particularly pleasant task of preparing a report on formation for our Provincial Council. I was the director of formation. I didn't really know where to start and my sense of inadequacy was making itself felt, but I didn't focus on it.

I leaned back in my chair and began to imagine myself standing before the Provincial Council. I wasn't there to give a report, however; I was there to receive a new assignment. My job was coming to an end and there were words of praise for my performance. But the words didn't affect my melancholy mood.

"Well, what next?" the provincial asked me smiling, his hands opening and then clasping in front of his chest. "What's available?" I asked. Several jobs were suggested, all of them of some prestige within our province. I thought I could do and enjoy any of them. But instead of naming one of the available jobs, I said somewhat sullenly, "For God's sake, gentlemen, give me a job that needs to be done well and will have some significance in your eyes."

The room was filled with consternation and some "What-ever-do-you-mean's." I told them that I thought I had done a good job at my previous tasks but that I wasn't sure anybody really gave a darn.

The scene faded amid protestations that no one doubted the significance of my contributions. But my doubt remained as I returned from my reverie and found myself still seated at my desk staring at the pages which needed to be compiled into a report.

I continued to sit there feeling very sad, allowing myself to sink into a new depth of feeling disconnected. I recognized clearly for the first time that much—even most—of my reason for doing what I did was to gain the approval of those who counted for me. And I had a hard time acknowledging and accepting that.

As I sat there my mind seemed involuntarily to retrace the path of my life back to the five years I had spent as novice master and then to the previous two years on the novitiate team. Had I done everything during that time merely to gain the approval of my peers and superiors and the affection and appreciation of the novices? I thought I had!

I was having a very difficult time accepting myself as I saw my self at that moment. The shallowness of my most ardent efforts became apparent. I wanted to run from it; I wanted to disengage from *me*! I despised myself to the point of almost becoming ill.

I allowed my eyelids to close. Tears moistened the edges of my eyelids. In the darkness within I struggled to accept what was now too obvious to deny. I had in fact gained the approval of my superiors, the respect of my peers and the affection and appreciation of many of the men who had been novices during those years of my young adulthood. Now it all felt like a sham. I wanted to be the person they approved, respected, loved and appreciated. But I knew I wasn't.

In that dark space somewhere near the core of myself, a light at first pierced and then spread. There began to dawn in that darkness the realization that God was not surprised at what I had just discovered. God had known all along! God was not having difficulty in accepting me; I was! God had accepted me in my neediness even as I was acting because of it. It was as if I had finally arrived at that hollow center of myself where God had been waiting for me, where God had been inviting me.

I cried softly. And I wiped my eyes. I sat there for a while and turned my chair to look out the window at the playground behind the school. Finally I smiled what I have always thought must be a wry sort of smile. And then it brightened into a broad smile and a laugh. "Come in," I called in response to the knock at the door. I swung around in the chair and looked at Jeannie, my secretary, standing in the doorway.

"Your door was closed. I thought maybe you had someone in here, but I couldn't hear any voices."

I don't remember what she wanted to talk about. But I remember listening to her and seeing her as if for the first time, probably because for the first time I wasn't trying to be somebody I thought could impress her.

My life didn't change because of that experience. But it was the first of many experiences of entering deeply into a moment of loneliness. The repeated entry into loneliness at more than its surface level has had a significant effect on my life.

I was an adult, reasonably well established within my province, before I began to realize that simple dissatisfactions are initial glimpses of my separateness, my incompleteness and my need for others; and that I can hold onto them instead of merely alleviating them by appropriate distraction. For me this deepening sense of loneliness involves allowing myself to recognize that much of my activity in life is motivated by my sense of disconnectedness from others.

When I see that I have gained the recognition and appreciation I sought for in my behavior, I can resent myself for having done my "generous deeds" motivated primarily by my unrecognized need for connectedness. And I can resent those whose care for me left me so needy. When I see that I haven't achieved the appreciation and recognition I long for, I can resent those who have failed to give it to me, as well as those who seem to have received those things I lack. Resentment is a defense against dealing with loneliness at a deeper level just as avoidance is at the surface level.

Any recognition of my neediness experienced here and now can call up emotional memories of past instances when my neediness was left unattended to. Resentments can be rekindled toward parents and siblings, peers and teachers, who always appeared stronger, more stable, better liked, less fragile and more caring of those around me than they were of me. My resentment may show itself in a low level hostility toward all those who have failed me and those who have received more of what I craved. Attacking people's character, instead of challenging their ideas, can be a clue that I am in touch with my own fragileness and am resenting it.

Loneliness has a sadness to it as it deepens, which may be felt only vaguely as dissatisfaction or a mild discomfort with what had been familiar and pleasing. Friends are liable to notice the sadness in me almost before I do.

The disconnectedness I feel in relation to those I miss or cannot reach can lead me to disengage even from other friends who are at hand and who invite me to enter their lives. "What's wrong?" one friend may ask another. "You look so sad."

I asked Jerry that question one night. He told me he was concerned about his mother's health and he was frustrated at not being able to rescue her from the circumstances which prevented her from seeking further and possibly better medical help. He told me he called a friend who had moved away recently, but the friend's voice did not reveal the enthusiasm he expected. "That's the way it is," he told himself. And he was sad.

Sadness like this marks a passage for mature people in the process of entering more deeply into loneliness. With our reluctant admission that things are in fact quite different from what we would prefer, we get our first frightening look at our own neediness. Not only is that moment's neediness unveiled, the neediness which has pervaded much of our care for family and friends throughout our lives is also unveiled. Our need for connectedness and the manner in which that need has pervaded our motivation gradually slips from beneath the veil. It is no work of art, this monument to our own self-preservation and need-fulfillment. But it is undeniably massive in stature.

Even when I avoid the resentment which leads to alienation from others, the impulse to cover my fragileness is strong. Engagement in familiar pursuits and patterns of active involvement with others in service, care, concern and friendship help me turn my back on the grotesque form I have uncovered. But I now know something about myself which no amount of covering or running away will let me forget.

There is an embarrassment in the recognition that I am so needy and that my neediness has dictated so much of my behavior. My conscious motivation may have been altruistic, my reward sought only from God. But the discovery of the idol to whom I have unconsciously paid such profound homage challenges even the foundations of the life I have lived. Now I must face myself and the God I have tried to serve. I need to come into the presence of God bringing with me the idol I've uncovered.

Then reconciliation can take place—reconciliation with myself, my need, my life up to now—and peace can return. Before my God, with my newly discovered neediness I can learn that I am the only one who is having a difficult time acknowledging and accepting who I am. If I stay there silent, I will know that already I have been acknowledged as needy and I have already been accepted by the God who made me that way. Once unmasked, my neediness is no longer an idol which I serve blindly. It is simply part of who I am.

All idolatry is making as an end what is given only as a means. My disconnectedness, my separateness, my incompleteness and my need for others is given to me at birth as a means to lead me to intimacy with others. Only when the unrecognized drive for connectedness motivates manipulative or mutilating behavior of ourselves or others, does neediness become destructive.

My recognition of the depth of my neediness in a moment of profound loneliness will allow me to "free the slaves," to let go of those for whom I care, because I don't want to use them for my own need-fulfillment. The sadness I feel will eventually give way to a new freedom for myself too, as I hear myself say of family and friends from whom I feel disconnected, "That's the way it *ought to be.*"

The new freedom is strange and uncomfortable at first. The monument I built to my own neediness does not disappear, but uncovered at last, it is no longer an idol demanding homage. It stands now as a silent reminder of a former bondage to which part of me will always be inclined to return.

But now I am free to choose to care for others because they need care, not just because I need to care for them; to engage others because they too feel disconnected, not just because I feel that way; even to forgive parents while seeing even more clearly their failures. Now I can leave others free to receive or reject the care I offer. Having unmasked my own idol I am less tempted to refashion others into my own image of who they should be, and I am less demanding that they respond to me as I anticipate and desire.

Knowing how fragile I am and having experienced acceptance by my God, I can now reach out to others whom I know are also fragile. Having been stripped of my own pretense of self-sufficiency, I can see beyond the pretense of others. I do not disdain them for their pretense, because I know how very fragile they sometimes feel in their apparent strength. My fragileness had not been tampered with by the God who acknowledged and accepted me; I will not tamper with theirs. I am able to connect with others now, not only out of my own unacknowledged need to do so, but because I appreciate much more deeply their need to be accepted as they are. I'm also less willing to be untrue to myself in an effort to have them connect with me. I will be less tempted to manipulate others to get the affection and appreciation I crave. I am prepared to directly pursue the fulfillment of my need for intimacy—to come together with others in a way that leaves us all intact.

Once I recognize and acknowledge and accept myself as

needing intimacy with others, I'm able to freely choose behaviors which will allow intimacy to arise. I'm able to deal
directly with my need for intimacy instead of seeking connectedness with others in mutual emotional dependence under the guise of care for them. My unacknowledged need-
fulfilling behavior, under whatever pretense, was a way I
drew sustenance from others as they may have drawn sustenance from me. The pleasure of it may have allowed it to
continue for quite some time. But sooner or later someone is
going to begin to feel drained or depleted or used.

In choosing behaviors which allow intimacy to evolve,
we no longer draw our sustenance from each other through
the protracted emotional dependence we may have established. Instead, we draw life from the relationship of intimacy which exists between us.

My need to connect with others is given to me by the
God who formed me in my mother's womb and allowed me
eventually to see the light of day. The need is given to me as
an impetus to establish intimate relationships with others.
Intimacy doesn't just happen because I have a need for it; it
is allowed to arise because of the behavior I choose in relating to other people. It is experienced only when two or more
persons fuse while each of them remains intact.

In this chapter I've revisited my experience of entering
into lonely moments and I've shared my reflection on that
experience. I'd like to conclude by summarizing what I have
learned through it all.

The initial glimpse I get of my separateness, incompleteness and neediness when I am alone and wanting to be
with others may frighten me so much that I try to avoid
lonely moments altogether. The attempts to avoid loneliness
lead only to isolation in my tower of pretended self-
sufficiency. I will experience my isolation even in the midst
of a crowd and, I suspect, even in bed with a spouse. Beneath the public or private performance is a person fearful
that he or she will not be accepted once the performance has
ended.

If, however, as a person frightened for his very existence, I enter more deeply and reflectively into that experience of loneliness which I glimpse, I may discover how fragile I really am. I might resent what I discover about myself and direct that resentment toward others.

If I face how fragile I am in my separateness I may be introduced into that meeting place of acknowledging and accepting myself where I will find comradeship with all other men and women and discover that I am one who is acknowledged and accepted by the God of us all. I emerge from that meeting place with a new solidarity with fragile sisters and brothers everywhere. I can connect with them without feeling that I have to be somebody else and without demanding that they be different. I may not like some of their behavior and they may not appreciate some of mine. But if I enter into my own experience of loneliness deeply enough to be in touch with the neediness which motivates much of my behavior, I may be able to recognize and sympathize with the fragileness which they protect and which prompts much of their behavior.

Intimacy is a special moment of life which I have experienced on a beach in southern California and with a friend who read me a story which revealed some of his deepest feelings; I need to lay myself open to moments of intimacy whenever they occur. Loneliness is another privileged moment of life; it prepares me for intimacy. It is mine because I am human.

Chapter 5
"Columns" and "Reservoirs"

For the past three or four years I've thought about my own experience of being sexual in the categories I've described in previous chapters. Although my experience is quite random and scattered, often confusing and sometimes frightening, the stories I tell myself about this experience are more logical and consistent. Perhaps that is the nature of stories—to help make sense of life. My thinking has also been influenced, and my experience given some order, by what several friends have said in conversations and in preparing and giving workshops on sexuality and celibacy.

I don't *experience* being sexual in the neat categories of biological urges, bio-psychological drives and personal/spiritual needs for intimacy that I use to *think* about my sexuality. I experience intimacy and other forms of connectedness with others as satisfying, and I experience loneliness as unpleasant. I'm glad to be with friends and frightened of feeling lonely. I'm sexually responsive in a physical way and usually don't know why. I find some people sexually attractive and respond emotionally to them when I don't even know their names. I walk away from time spent with a friend and feel whole but not elated, and I don't even try to explain to myself why I feel that way. I experience being sexual with all its urges, drives, needs, fantasies, impulses, emotions and dreams. I have, however, thought a lot about what I've experienced.

It seems to me that I experience a very irrational and impulsive side to my being sexual—a jumble of urges and drives, fantasies, impulses, feelings, dreams, physical responses, attractions, satisfactions. Until recently I have tried to explain to myself *why* I experience this impulsive side of being sexual. Or I tell myself stories about what some irrational impulse means or what will almost inevitably follow it.

If I were to dream of hugging and kissing the wife of a very good friend, I could "explain" that she had been on my mind during the preceding week, or that I'm lonely and haven't been doing anything to deal with it, or that celibacy is getting to me, or maybe that I need a little romantic activity or even some genital involvement with someone.

If I were to get erections for just about any conceivable reason or for no apparent reason, I could tell myself that it must be spring, or a full moon, or that celibacy is getting to me, or maybe my prostate is enlarging, or I must be more sexually responsive than most men.

If I found myself fantasizing about genital sex or romantic activity or a tender encounter with three or four different people at the same time, I could tell myself that I must be a pervert, or celibacy is getting to me, or my sexual desires must be the strongest in the world.

If I found myself fantasizing or dreaming about any kind of romantic or genital involvement with another man, I could tell myself that I must be homosexually oriented, that celibacy is getting to me, that I'm not having enough contact with the women in my life, that seminary life as an adolescent has ruined me, or any number of other explanations for *why* I was experiencing what I was, *what it meant* and *what would almost inevitably follow*.

I'm pretty sure it's because I've had a lot of opportunity to listen to other men and women—celibate, married and single—that I've concluded that there is no readily available explanation for why a person experiences being sexual in a particular way. I've also concluded that what people tell themselves about the meaning of their experience and what must inevitably follow from it depends on the information and misinformation they've received from others and the expectations which have been created in their own minds.

For now, I've decided that human sexuality has a thoroughly irrational and impulsive side to it that *cannot be easily explained*, that *means no more than that one is sexual*, and that *has no inevitable consequences* to it at all. I've also concluded that an experience of the irrational and impulsive side of their sexuality can lead married people, single people and celibate people to suspect that there is something about marriage, the single life or the celibate commitment which is wrong for them. And many people—married, single and intending to remain single, single and hoping to marry some day, and celibate—regard their sexuality as something beyond their control. Those who regard their life commitment as having given meaning and direction to their sexual urges and drives usually regard anything about their experience of sexuality which doesn't fit easily with their commitment as unfriendly and inimical to that commitment. Some have concluded that their sexual urges and drives are uncontrollable, and any experience of their urgency is only an invitation to seek some sexual activity, even if only for recreation and relief. The most common expression I've heard from celibate men who are feeling sexually responsive is, "Maybe I should masturbate now and get it over with instead of struggling for a few days and then masturbating anyway."

The images people have of their sexuality vary greatly. Two images which I have found stereotypical are "the column" and "the reservoir."

In speaking of our irrational and impulsive experience of sexuality with Jerry, I arrived at the image of the column. These sexual urges, drives, imaginings and feelings seem at times to be a huge and powerful column rising up within us. Next to the column is a small gallows-shaped control station which is the rational aspect of our personality—our insight and free choice. This miniature control station is supposed to regulate our sexual behavior, to hold back the force of the column and direct its impulses into channels that are acceptable and compatible with our life commitments.

In discussing this image with another friend, we realized that it was not expansive enough to capture everyone's experience. Another "typical" image is that of a reservoir of immense urges, drives, imaginings and impulses contained by a gate or a dam. The banks of the reservoir are so much higher than the dam that it seems almost inevitable that the pent-up water will rise at times and overflow the gate which is supposed to control the irrational and impulsive sexual drives and urges.

Whatever the image, the underlying assumptions are frequently these: First, the irrational and impulsive urges are strong and unpredictable and most likely unfriendly toward whatever order and meaning a person may have already given to his or her sexual experience; second, the control system for sexuality is not equal to the strength of the impulses; third, sexual behavior flows directly from the impulsive and irrational urges and drives which in turn give shape and direction to a person's life despite the workings of the control station or gate. I have never heard anyone just sit down and say "I have these three assumptions about my sexuality," and then proceed to elaborate on them. Rather, as I have listened to people talk about their experience of being sexual, I have heard these assumptions expressed in several different ways.

The first assumption is that these irrational and impulsive sexual urges and drives are strong, unpredictable and most likely unfriendly. I agree that they are strong and unpredictable, but I no longer think they are unfriendly. Most of us tend to hide our experience of our sexual urges and drives from everybody, including ourselves. We seem to feel we're better off not even looking at them unless they become so urgent that they demand our attention. If we find ourselves physically or emotionally responsive to a person or a situation, we tend to regard that as a problem we're going to have to address someday. Most of us have mechanisms in place by which we manage to ignore or deny, for a little while at least, the presence of any sexual urges or drives which we find unacceptable. Anything in the column or reservoir which is not already understood by our insight and controlled by our free choice is denied consciously or unconsciously, or is hastily assigned a meaning which we consider acceptable.

I have a hunch that a lot of what psychologists and psychiatrists deal with is ignored, denied, repressed and misinterpreted sexual urges and drives. Anything in the column which seems to loom larger than the control station, or anything in the reservoir which seems to swell the waters to a level higher than the gate might be better unacknowledged. "Maybe if I pretend it isn't there, it won't act up!"

The second assumption is that the strength of the control station is not equal to the force of the impulsive urges and drives. I don't agree with that assumption. Doubt about our ability to understand and to make choices concerning our irrational and impulsive urges and drives often leads us to ignore or deny them. "I'd better not get involved in something I can't handle." The unexamined urges and drives intimidate us, not because of their great strength, but because we *presume* that no force can withstand them.

The third assumption is that our sexual behavior flows directly from the irrational and impulsive urges and drives, which in turn give shape and direction to our lives. I don't agree with this assumption either. Many people believe that to acknowledge our sexual urges and drives is to act them out. They see only two options: repress them or act them out. "If I am attracted to someone, I can either ignore it and hope it goes away, or act on it."

The absence of such urges is also thought to give direction to a person's life. "I no longer feel anything for you" is the reason given for dissolving many marriages. "I don't feel romantically or sexually attracted to anyone so maybe I have a vocation to religious life or the priesthood." The reasoning goes that we can only hope that whatever is in our column or reservoir will remain hidden there. Or if it does reveal itself, that it will be compatible with the commitments we have already made.

Many regard the on-going recognition of urges and drives as reason enough to change commitments, even if those commitments were made for life. "I made a poor choice when I decided to marry you. If I had known then what I know now, I never would have made that commitment," some say. Or, "When I chose a celibate life I was too young, and I didn't know what it would be like to fall in love. Now I know that I never should have made a celibate commitment." Once aware of an impulsive and irrational sexual urge which we previously ignored or denied, we may feel that in order to be "true" to ourselves we must at least seriously consider leaving our spouse or taking one.

Once articulated these assumptions seem too obviously flawed to be influential in anybody's life. But they are seldom clearly thought. When shared by enough people, these assumptions are lived out by just about everyone because "that's just the way it is." Let me give some examples of these assumptions as they operate in people's lives:

Len is a candidate for a community of religious men. He is living in a residence for pre-novitiate students while he finishes his senior year of college. Jennifer is a pre-med student at the same school. She has ruled out marriage until after medical school.

At a parish Thanksgiving party Len meets Jennifer and dances with her several times. Even though she came to the party with a group of friends, she accepts Len's invitation to drive her home.

By Christmas vacation Len and Jennifer go to lunch together several times. They find each other very attractive.

During the spring break, Len finds living in the pre-novitiate house almost intolerable; he is always thinking of Jennifer who is in Florida for vacation. When she returns to school, Len tells her that he is considering dropping out of the pre-novitiate program, even though he has already applied for admission to novitiate.

Eventually Len speaks to one of the members of the religious community, stating that he wants to withdraw his application for the novitiate and leave the pre-novitiate program at the end of the school year. He tells his director that he feels very dishonest, and that he now knows religious life is not for him. Even though Jennifer isn't interested in marriage, he wants to continue to date her in the hope that she will change her mind.

Asked how he knows religious life is not for him, Len responds that he feels dissatisfied at the pre-novitiate house and enlivened when he is with Jennifer.

"But you don't even know if Jennifer will spend her life with you," his director cautions him. "You're trying to convince her to do something she has decided not to do."

"But I feel so much affection for her; I love her," Len protests. "She's the best thing that ever happened to me. And besides, even if she won't marry me, I can't go to novitiate knowing all the time that I'd rather be with her."

The director is dismayed. Len has been interested in religious life since his junior year of high school. He has pursued that goal through his years of college. He has dated and has had many women his own age as friends for years.

"How can you decide that your attraction to Jennifer means that religious life is not for you?"

"I just know it," Len says. "I've never felt like this toward anyone before."

It may be a poor time for Len to enter novitiate. He seems to have some real issues to work through before he can reasonably make a vocational choice. But he is in fact making a vocational choice in abandoning his pursuit of religious life, and he is doing so on the assumption that he has no control over his behavior because of bio-psychological sexual drives—his fascination with Jennifer. He assumes that his life must be shaped by his powerful sexual attraction for her. Jennifer isn't interested in pursuing life with Len, but Len feels that he can change that. Maybe she too will be overpowered by her feelings and revise her plans.

He knows he cannot change Jennifer's mind right now, and he feels quite certain that he cannot change his behavior toward her.

Len's decision to abandon his pursuit of religious life may be disappointing to his director and to others. But that's Len's decision. What I find disappointing is Len's telling himself that the decision is all but made for him by what he has discovered in his column. It is not only his decision to leave the pre-novitiate program which is influenced by his assumption that his sexual impulses *must* be followed; since the Thanksgiving dance he has made decisions about his behavior toward Jennifer. By choosing to pursue Jennifer he has gradually withdrawn from involvement in the pre-novitiate program. And he assumes that it has all just happened because of behavior which has stemmed from a sexual drive in him over which he has no control. In many ways he sees his life taking shape before him and feels in some ways a willing victim of his own sexual urges and drives.

Luanne is a religious sister. She has been in her community for 19 years. She is 41 years old. During the four years she has worked at the chancery office of the diocese, she has had quite a bit of contact with the marriage tribunal and its proceedings. Her friend Peter, who has an apartment in the building where Luanne lives with two sisters of her community, got a civil divorce four years ago. He gained custody of his son Duane who was a 3-year-old at the time of the divorce. Luanne has been advising Peter on how to go about applying for an annulment.

Luanne doesn't feel very close to either of the two sisters

she lives with, but occasionally she gets together with Joan, another sister of her community who is a good friend. During a recent visit with Joan, Luanne confides that she expects to confront a vocational choice a year or two in the future. She is getting more and more attracted to Peter and Duane. Joan is dismayed and talks much more strongly to her friend than usual.

Luanne admits to Joan that what started as a kind gesture toward Peter, who knew nothing about the process of seeking an annulment, had developed into a friendship and that now she is feeling more and more romantic toward him. Yes, she sees Peter several times a week for lunch or in the evening. Yes, they did begin a year or two ago to get physical in their expression of affection for each other. No, she never said anything to the sisters with whom she lives. Yes, Duane likes her as much as she likes him; he asked his father once if Luanne would be his new mother.

Luanne thinks of Peter most of every day. She has shared with Peter her own personal struggles and dissatisfactions with her life as a religious. And Peter has spoken at length about the sadness of his marriage. Until today Luanne has not shared with anyone in her community that her friendship with Peter has gone from wanting to help him, to feeling a lot of affection for him and his son, to very passionate romantic activity on occasion. Each time there has been romantic behavior between them, Luanne has resolved that she will not lose control again. Because of her resolve, she has told herself that there is no need to mention it to anyone. It's not yet out of hand, she says, because she has gone further with other men and has managed to break off those relationships.

At today's get-together with Joan, Luanne gives her friend the outline of the relationship with Peter in order to prepare her "just in case anything happens" and to get advice from her on how to deal with her own powerful feelings for Peter and her lack of enthusiasm for religious life.

Luanne confides to her friend that she suspects her upbringing in her strict Catholic family and her early years in religious life did nothing to help her discover and explore her
sexuality. Now it seems to be demanding real exploration,
and it's just possible that a major vocational decision is
"down the road."

Joan is frank and firm. She's shocked, disappointed and
hurt that Luanne has never mentioned this long-time relationship to her. Joan has a lot of affection and admiration
for Luanne, but suddenly she feels very left out of Luanne's
life. "Luanne," she says as she prepares to get into her car to
return home, "the vocational decision you talk about isn't
two or three years down the road. It's as close as what you
decide to do tonight."

In my opinion, Luanne is giving too much weight to
the force of her biological and bio-psychological sexual
drives. She has been doing so for years and in relationships
with several men before Peter. She has already failed to stop
the urges and drives from finding expression in her behavior.
She has become accustomed to thinking that when she feels
romantic she must act that way. She is telling herself that no
matter what commitments she may have made, her life will
possibly take a different shape because of what she feels for
Peter. She has made herself a bystander to her own life, just
waiting to see what will happen and preparing her closest
friend for the possibility that what will happen will be disappointing to her. She has told herself she must wait and see
where her genital sexual urges and romantic drives will take
her.

Kevin is 35 years old. He is a religious in temporary
vows. Prior to his interest in religious life he accumulated a
great deal of job experience in the metropolitan school dis-
trict of his home town. Both of Kevin's parents migrated as
children with their own parents from Mississippi to a northern industrial city in search of work. Kevin's parents had

been raised staunch Catholics, and they had raised him that way.

Kevin could have been appointed an assistant principal of a high school; instead, he decides to take a leave from the school system and explore his long-standing interest in religious life. He dated in high school and college, and had been engaged, but he broke off the engagement two years prior to applying for religious life.

During his novitiate year Kevin finds himself very attracted sexually to one of his younger classmates, but he dismisses his attraction and attributes it to the fact that he lives now in a predominantly male environment. After two years in temporary vows he meets William, a man his own age, at the counselling center where he does some part-time ministry. William makes some sexual advances toward Kevin, and on the third occasion Kevin goes home with him where they go to bed together.

Kevin can't bring himself to talk to his director about the incident, and only after several months of seeing William regularly and occasional genital encounters with him does he tell his director that he is in love. He says he has fallen in love with a girl at work. He talks about his feelings for his friend, always leading his director to believe his friend is Nancy. He speaks with the other members of his community somewhat frankly about his love affair with Nancy, and the vocational crisis it has occasioned. Kevin always translated the advice he got about his relationship with Nancy into terms which gave direction to his dealings with William.

Tonight Kevin has an appointment with his director, and he is going to tell him the whole truth. He has already decided to leave the religious order and to move in with William. He has traced his own sexual history and is going to share that with his director. All during high school he ignored his attraction for other boys and dated girls. He broke off the engagement he had because he just didn't feel he was ready for marriage. Now he can see that he just didn't have enough romantic feelings for his fiancee. He simply put all sexual relationships out of his mind and buried himself in his work. After he had met a priest of the religious order, he found himself attracted to the possibility of being a religious and a priest, so he had applied for admission. The rest of the story his director knows.

Kevin is convinced he is now going to take the only honest way—leave the order and move in with William. He hates to leave the order and his brothers in religious life among whom he has been very popular. He fears the reaction of his family, and he has decided not to tell them about William. But, granted his feelings and his sexual history and his emotional involvement with William, he can see no other option which would allow him to feel honest with himself.

Kevin's decision bothers me. He has ignored and denied so much over the years of growing up, and he has been dishonest with himself and with those who were closest to him. He has amassed a large collection of stories to tell himself about his experience, and now he decides he will be honest and leave the order! He is sincerely responding to the stories he has told himself, but his honesty is based on the assumption that he cannot do anything but follow out his sexual inclinations, and that they must now give shape to his life.

Len, Luanne and Kevin are fictional characters, their situations composites of things I have heard from many people. Most of us know at least a small portion of someone's story—as well as our own—and may be able to recognize the dynamics these fictional characters experienced. They strike me as very similar to those experienced by millions of people who meet, fall in love and move toward marriage to each other. Some, of course, see no need of marriage and move into romantic and genital relationships without getting married. But there is usually even for them some sense of mating. For all of them, the assumptions are these: the irrational and impulsive sexual urges and drives are strong, probably stronger than any control they may want to exert over their behavior; the urges and drives need to be acted out, and their lives will take shape because of the behavior *demanded* by the urges and drives. The same dynamics and assumptions seem to be active for countless married people who find themselves responding emotionally to someone other than their spouses.

Similar dynamics and assumptions have been enshrined in literature, classic and modern—Guinevere and Lancelot of *Camelot* and Father Ralph DuBricassart of *The Thornbirds* standing merely as representatives of them all. The expectations and assumptions most people seem to have about their sexuality are firmly in place, strongly reinforced in the media, and rarely examined or challenged.

In real life and in literature there is a chronology in the way people deal with their sexual urges and drives. Ignorance of the existence of such urges and drives is the first natural state we experience. But when the urges and drives begin to make themselves felt and ignorance begins to give way, we tend at first to try to remain ignorant by ignoring them. We pretend we don't see them, much as we pretend not to see someone in a crowd whom we really don't want to speak to.

Sexual urges and drives, like all other aspects of life can be ignored only by focusing our attention on something else. Immersion in work or sports or "noble pursuits" provides a handy way of ignoring our sexual urges and drives.

If I am ignoring my sexuality, and it begins to make itself felt, I might hastily assign some acceptable meaning to whatever I am experiencing.

When that won't work any more, we tend to deny the existence of our urges and drives, even to ourselves.

A sign that I am denying my sexual urges and drives (and perhaps neglecting my need for intimacy) is rationalizing romantic or genital behavior which is incompatible with who I am and with commitments I have made—or in the case of single people who are having intercourse, with commitments they haven't made. When I'm at the stage of denying what I can no longer ignore, I act out in questionable ways what I don't want to acknowledge, and I rationalize what I'm doing as "good for someone else" or "the way it ought to be" for everybody. What I do may possibly be good for another and may be a healthier way of acting than is generally practiced, but if I'm denying my urges and drives and needs, I'll tell myself that a little nudity is good for so-and-so, for instance, or a display of affection is healthy, and never admit that I *like* to be naked and I *like* to receive and give affection. I can take as a clue that I'm denying my sexual urges when I protest that what I'm doing is right and good without admitting that it is also fun.

If we get beyond ignoring and denying our irrational and impulsive sexual urges and drives, we may acknowledge them. We may indeed feel we have been forced to do so because of their urgency. We are at the stage of acknowledging our urges and drives when we begin to freely choose to act them out even if doing so is contrary to what we believe is compatible with commitments we have made. Forgetting that life-commitments are a part of who we are, we act contrary to them and tell ourselves that we must be "true" to ourselves by giving expression to our urges and drives. Acknowledging sexual urges and romantic inclinations after a long time of ignoring and denying them is particularly dangerous to commitments already made.

Often acknowledging our urges and drives is as far as we go. Yet a fourth step is required for human sexuality; namely, to accept or own what we find in our columns and reservoirs. When we tell ourselves that we have to be true to ourselves—and that means waiting to see what shape our life will take, quite independent of life commitments already made—we're acknowledging our sexual urges and drives without accepting and owning them. Accepting and owning our sexuality with all of its irrational and impulsive elements means we take charge of its modulation or moderation with our insight and freedom.

All behavior stems from decisions we make, not simply from our urges and drives and feelings. If we decided to ignore or deny what's in our columns or reservoirs, we give up control of our urges and drives. Our so-called uncontrollable sexual behavior flows from our decision to ignore or deny our urges and drives. It's a bit like deciding to ignore traffic signals or to deny that they exist, and then blaming the accident we have on the other person or on the power of our own car's engine. In fact, our life takes its shape because of the behaviors we choose from the options which are open to us; only if we *choose* to ignore or deny or to give free reign to our irrational and impulsive urges and drives do they give shape to our lives because of the choices we have made.

My own assumptions about sexuality, my own as well as everybody else's experience, is that I have irrational and impulsive urges, drives, fears and fantasies and they are friendly. I assume that I am supposed to discover the meaning and purpose of those urges and drives, and that I am supposed to decide what I want to do about them. The options open to me are to *ignore* them or to *deny* them, to *acknowledge* them and wait to see where acting them out will carry me, or to *own* them and to decide if and how I will act them out.

Should I choose to act them out, I can do so in romantic and genital behavior. But I have no instinctual regulatory device within me which directs and gives meaning to my behavior. I have to use my insight—aided by the insights of other human beings in the traditions of human culture—to discover what that meaning is, and I have to use my freedom to choose behaviors which can achieve that meaning. Or, of course, I can choose romantic and genital behaviors which in no way achieve the meaning and purpose of human sexuality.

As an individual human being, I cannot give a strictly personal meaning to my own romantic and genital sexual behavior any more than I can give a strictly personal meaning to the words I use. There is a cultural meaning to words. The sounds uttered may be arbitrary to some extent, but the words have been given a meaning by the culture which shares them. "I love you" sounds different in Italian and French and Greek. But whatever the cultural sounds, the meaning cannot be changed by individuals. What is true of words is also true of clothing and touch—two other media for conveying romantic and genital messages. The more private the encounter and the more intimate the relationship between people, the more personal can be the meaning of language, clothing, touch and romantic and genital behavior between them. But even in the privacy of two very intimately related friends, the cultural meaning is present and the personal meanings I may wish to convey must be compatible with the cultural expressions I choose.

Let me try to put some flesh on what I'm saying. I cannot show up in jeans and T-shirt at a formal dinner given by my closest friend and rely on the personal intimacy between us—how fully we have allowed each to know the other—to contradict the meaning of my behavior. My friend may know of my love and appreciation for him or her, but there is a cultural meaning to clothing which this personal knowledge cannot overcome in that public setting. In private we can give our personal meaning to the clothing we wear, but not in public. Between close friends language can take on added meaning, but that meaning will be lost in a group of strangers.

Romantic behavior too has meanings which cannot be escaped. Whatever the behavior in a given culture that has romantic meaning, as a member of that culture I am bound by the cultural meaning of that behavior. Romantic behavior suggests something. It suggests that I want to pursue with you the possibility of our choosing each other as mates. If I engage in romantic behavior with you and do not intend to pursue that possibility, I am lying to you just as surely as if I say "I love you" in order to betray you. Romantic behavior which excludes the intention to pursue a more lasting relationship with you will eventually result in your being hurt. There is no promise in romantic behavior, just a suggestion. Many couples have broken off their romantic relationship because one has decided that the other has been suggesting they get married long enough. Eventually one asks, "Are you serious in what you suggest or not?"

Genital behavior does more than suggest something; it *promises*. Intercourse promises to be there for each other in the future. I may not intend that meaning when I engage in intercourse with another, but I cannot escape the meaning implied in the behavior. For intercourse to have meaning, the promise implied in the behavior needs to be explicitly intended and stated. Once that commitment is made, my partner and I can enjoy the fun of sex together because we are not having fun at the other's expense. We can have intercourse for recreation because we intend and have publicly stated to each other that we mean what we say in our behavior.

Intercourse says, "I will be there for you in the future." If enough of us engage in genital sexual behavior and do not intend to be there for each other in the future, we all suffer because we all are losing the meaning which the behavior has in itself. Intercourse for recreation without a commitment to each other is not *human* sexuality.

That romantic activity suggests something and intercourse promises something are stories I tell myself. They are stories which I have arrived at because of the attention I have paid to my own experience of being sexual and because of the listening I have done to married couples, single and celibate people, and especially to unmarried mothers. Other people tell themselves different stories about romantic and genital behavior. In the privacy of their own relationships with another human being many believe they can give their own meaning to romantic and genital expressions and completely exclude and escape all cultural meanings. A society which adopts as its stance the position that sex is a private affair—that it is permissible for individuals to give their own meaning to romantic and genital behavior completely exclusive of all cultural meaning—will have to deal with tremendous human wreckage. A society which opts to deal with the wreckage instead of insisting on maintaining the cultural meanings of romantic and genital behavior will see the disintegration of its stability and the depletion of its resources.

My own culture and society are currently choosing to chart the data concerning increasing sexual behavior by its young, an escalating number of rapes, an incredible divorce rate, unmarried mothers and unwanted children, broken hearts and broken homes, uncountable abortions and psychological and emotional problems in an increasing number of its members as a result of meaningless sexual behavior, and it isn't telling itself any story at all about the meaning of human sexuality. It simply tries to educate people on ways to engage in sexual behavior without any consequences, and it prepares professionals to deal with those whose lives are permanently marred because of meaningless sexual behavior, their own, their neighbors' or their ancestors'.

Human sexual behavior has a meaning which can be neglected or circumvented only to the detriment of individual human persons and to the society which they make up. Human sexual behavior which meets neither the need for the species to continue nor the need of each person for intimacy falls short of the meaning it is meant to have. The effect on a society of its condoning meaningless sexual activity will be exactly the same as the effect the confusion of language had on the people of Babel. When language no longer had meaning, the society crumbled. When sexual activity has no meaning, the same result is predictable. A society which insists on the right of each individual to engage in sexual behavior and to give sexual activity his or her own meaning exclusive of a cultural meaning has placed explosives around the foundations on which it stands.

I'm glad for the irrational and impulsive side of my sexuality. And I'm glad for the moderating influence of my insight and freedom. I have discovered that my sexuality is friendly. I can trust it. My column alone cannot be trusted only because it is incomplete, not because it is unfriendly. It is that in me which impels me to come together with others. Thus attracted to others, I can choose how I will behave toward them. I can choose to behave in a way which merely gratifies my biological urges and bio-psychological drives, or I can choose to behave in ways which benefit the other and which open to us the possibility of an intimacy to develop which will meet our needs. My attraction to others is not the only possible motivation for behaving toward them in ways which benefit them, but it is certainly one of the motivations I have experienced.

I presume that what I will continue to discover in my column will be surprising, frightening at times, mystifying, exciting, and always give my control station something to think about and play with and make decisions about—yes, and even to write books about! What I find will always, I suppose, present me with options to consider and choices to make.

Chapter 6
Relationships

"Relationships between people *can* be personal," I told myself as I sat in my parked car in front of an airline terminal awaiting the arrival of a visitor. What caused my reflection was the scene I had just witnessed. A Bronco wagon pulled up, but instead of pulling over to the curb it stopped in the right lane. The driver, a man of perhaps 35, signalled to a woman of the same age, who approached the curb with a suitcase in each hand and a shoulder bag. She was accompanied by a girl of about ten, also carrying a piece of luggage.

The man got out of the wagon, walked swiftly around to the rear and began opening the door for the luggage. The woman stood on the curb with the little girl beside her. I couldn't hear their conversation but I watched what seemed to be a relationship which was not very personal.

He smiled, particularly at the little girl. She smiled and waved a restrained little wave at him. The woman looked harried. She set the bags on the curb and began pointing to the man that he should back the vehicle into the space next to the curb. The man's smile fell, and he tightened the muscle of his left cheek bringing that side of his mouth up and to the side. He cast a quick glance to the sky and looked down immediately. He closed the tailgate, returned to the driver's seat and backed the car into the space.

A second time he got out opened the rear door, fetched

the luggage from the curb and placed it in the back of the vehicle. The little girl handed him the bag she carried and they smiled at each other. The woman walked to the front door of the wagon and motioned the girl into the front seat. The man closed the rear door, slamming the tire rack into place with just a little more force than was required. The woman got into the front seat and pulled the door closed. Through the rear window of their vehicle I could see the little girl's head looking at the man, the woman looking straight ahead, and the driver looking in the outside mirror and over his left shoulder as he pulled out into traffic.

What I had witnessed reminded me that relationships between persons *can be* personal. It also gave evidence that even in marriage the relationships can be merely functional.

I've never been married, so my notions about the relationship between spouses and between parents and children concern only the possibilities of those relationships. I know myself to be realistic enough to recognize that possibilities can develop into actualities only with a lot of hard work and often with a lot of luck.

But more is possible than what I witnessed between the man and the woman at the airport. I was born with a need to connect with other human beings. Initially that connection was simply functional on my part; I needed food and nurture. Those who parented me perhaps responded emotionally and even experienced a very personal commitment to my survival and well being. But there was no mutuality of emotional response or personal commitment. I would have to be taught to respond in emotional and personal ways as my capacity to do so awakened.

My need and my awakened capacities for connecting with other human beings are meant to develop to the point of human maturity where intimacy with other human beings becomes possible. The urge, the drive and the need to connect with other human beings are all part of my being sexual. It allows me to connect with other human beings in relationships beyond the functional. But my urges, drives and needs do not of themselves assure that I will attain the personal connectedness for which they are given. I need to learn and then to choose behavior which will allow the connectedness to occur.

Functionally I remain connected throughout most of my life or I would not survive. I too need a ride from the airport frequently. And I go to our dining room three times a day expecting, without much thought, that someone has prepared a meal or at least bought the wherewithal for me to make a breakfast. People grow and sell food and make and distribute products or perform services which I require for survival. I produce or perform myself because someone needs my product or service. But there is nothing in those producer-consumer exchanges which in themselves relates me to another person. At that level we merely fill functions and roles.

Being sexual opens for me the possibility of relating to others in ways beyond the functional. Being sexual in a uniquely human way opens the possibility that my functional as well as my genital and romantic relationships can achieve personal meaning. Not only are our roles and functions related so that we touch each other in filling those roles and performing those functions; not only can we touch each other and connect our bodies in genital contact; not only can we respond emotionally to each other and touch each other through our affection; we can connect as persons in intimate relationships in which our spirits touch each other.

If we achieve and sustain the capacity for intimacy— that uniquely human possibility of being sexual—we can transform our functional relationships and our genital and romantic relationships, and achieve a uniquely human meaning. In filling our required roles and functions, in intercourse and in romantic pursuits, it is possible for our spirits, our persons, to touch and to nourish each other as persons.

I think I have just said the same thing in three different

ways and I meant to do so, I am frankly enchanted with the possibilities which being sexual in our unique human ways opens up to us. I am also saddened by the pain and disappointment I see all around me—in married couples, in single men and women and in celibate priests and religious—when people settle for functional, genital and romantic relationships which are not also personal. At times it seems as though people are slowly dying of malnutrition in the midst of plenty.

Our initial relationships in infancy and in childhood were functional by necessity. In adolescence we experienced a maturing genital awakening and found ourselves stimulated by others. By the time we left our parental home we had relationships with friends and associates, perhaps leaving our childhood home because we had or hoped to develop relationships with someone or some group to whom we thought we could commit ourselves in an adult pursuit. The entire process seemed more to happen to us than to be something we set out to do.

From what I have observed of my three brothers and of many others suggests that they were cared for in the family home, and this care awakened and educated their own emotional and ethical ability to care for others. Friendships and other kinds of relationships developed outside the home, and eventually they met "the right one" to whom they were willing and able to make a romantic and genital commitment in marriage. It all seemed to happen naturally and effortlessly.

My own experience was similar. To this day I am unsure just why I wanted to go to the seminary, except that Sister Dorothy and Father McCollow indicated that it was a real possibility for me if I wanted to pursue it. Going to the seminary was not a definitive leaving of my folks' home, of course. I established relationships outside the family, and eventually decided that I wanted to be a Capuchin and to commit my life to that group of men whose life appealed to me. For me it happened with the same apparent natural ease as seemed to be the case for my brothers.

In fact we were led to make our commitment, not because the person or the lifestyle was *so* attractive and had *so much* meaning for us, but because of a series of behaviors which we found it rather easy to choose because of the attraction and the meaning we experienced. Having made a life commitment—or even a temporary one in religious vows—we can mistakenly think we have reached our destination. In fact we have simply decided what we will pursue for the rest of our lives. Our *commitment* to the pursuit must replace the *enticement* as our motivation for further growth.

In marriage, the genital urge and the romantic drive which led people to their commitment need not and ought not cease. Married couples need to continue to choose behaviors toward one another which will develop their committed relationship in a personally intimate experience of romance and genital sex. Those committed to celibacy or to the single life need to continue to choose behaviors which will develop a greater appreciation of the life they have chosen. All of us need to learn and to choose behaviors which will develop the relationships we have undertaken to the point that they ripen into personally intimate relationships. Only by doing so will we achieve the fulfillment the lifestyle promised when we began to pursue it.

All of this can seem as obvious as my statement that relationships between people can be personal. But my experience suggests that people are strongly inclined to abdicate to someone else the responsibility for their own happiness, particularly their happiness in relationships. A lot of us wait for other people to behave in ways which will make our relationships with them fulfilling. And that's a mistake.

In workshops that Jerry, Jan and I give, we encourage a high level of self-awareness and invite the participants to disclose to their partners as much of that self-awareness as they want. For the fourth and final topic we invite the participants to explore relationships. We begin by asking them to look at their behavior during the week.

The only dynamics we use in our workshops are self-awareness, self-disclosure and hearing. It seems to make little difference whether one chooses friends or strangers for partners. It does seem to make a great deal of difference that each one has the choice to make. Members of those groups which are already constituted and within which there are already patterns of relationships seem to get less out of the workshops than do members of the groups which come together for the first time.

All those experiences have led me to conclude that most of us attribute the success in establishing and maintaining satisfying personal relationships to what someone else does or fails to do. In fact, the possibilities of personally intimate relationships arising and being sustained are dependent on our own behavior!

Many of us think that establishing a good personal relationship depends on what is inside the participants. I believe a relationship does not depend on what goes on inside each person, but on what is communicated, either directly or indirectly, between and among them. What goes on within each person defines and limits the *possibilities* any personal relationship will have. Whether or not a relationship will actually be established and maintained depends on the behavior of the participants. The satisfaction people feel in their personal relationships increases as the disclosure of what goes on inside of them becomes more direct and the hearing of the other person's disclosure becomes more accurate. Direct self-disclosure and attentive listening also increases the clarity of the relationship and the ability to manage it, to pursue its development, and to specify its nature.

Whether we have committed ourselves to relationships to other human beings in marriage or religious life or the priesthood, our personalities do not guarantee the success of the relationships, nor do the circumstances which bring contrary commitments into our lives or keep them from arising. It is not someone else's efforts which make us leave our commitment or keep us faithful to the pursuit of the development of what we began. It is our choice of behaviors and the skill we exercise in those behaviors which will predict our success or failure.

Whichever of the lasting life-forms we have chosen to pursue—marriage, celibate life or single life—we bring to that life our biological urges, our bio-psychological drives and our personal/spiritual need for intimacy. Our sexuality opens to us the possibility of entering into permanent or temporary personal relationships with other human beings. No relationship will be fulfilling unless it includes behaviors which allow intimacy to arise. Intimacy will be found wherever we enter a relationship in which personal fusing with another is experienced, as well as a counterpointing of personalities. A personal relationship *is* an intimate relationship.

I don't think there is a different kind of *intimacy* for married people than there is for celibates or singles. Different kinds of *relationships* take their shape from the way intimacy is experienced and expressed. There are intimate genital relationships, intimate romantic relationships, and I suppose one could speak of intimate spiritual relationships, though I tend to think that because a relationship is intimate it is of its nature spiritual. Even some functional relationships are intimate. What makes them all intimate is that the interaction between two or more people allows the personalities of each to fuse with the other while each one remains intact. No one is dominated, subjugated, used, abused, manipulated, or obliterated in any way by coming together with the other or others. Intimate relationships are always personal, and I am convinced that they arise because of certain behaviors on the part of all who are involved, namely: self-awareness, self-disclosure and hearing of each other.

Relationships with others start with self-awareness. I

have found that my relationships improve in their quality and in the satisfaction I derive from them almost in proportion to the solitude I experience in my life. If I take the time alone to allow my thoughts to formulate clearly; if I take the time alone to reflect on what I have experienced and how I have behaved and how I have felt; if I take the time alone to recognize the attitudes and assumptions which I have perhaps unknowingly espoused, I find that in coming together with friends, and even with strangers, I am able more easily to reveal to them the data of my life.

Part, but by no means all, of what happens for me as I sit in my easy chair and write whatever comes to mind is an increased clarity in my understanding of myself. So if I want to disclose myself to another, I am more equipped to do so. But more than that happens for me. It is in my moments alone that I get in touch with how fragile I really am. Most of my hours are spent with others. I usually look pretty good in that public forum; at least I try to. I seem to most people to be rather competent and insightful, even handy at a few things. I look pretty magnanimous, accommodating, enthusiastic, pleasant. And those are the impressions which are reflected back to me by those who experience me in public. If I don't take time alone, I lose track of how fragile, mean and cheap, how unsure of myself, how self-serving even in my service to others, and how frightened and confused I also am. My ability to feel compassion for those people in my life who don't always look so good depends on my being in touch with my own fragileness; my ability to see beyond the surface of those who seem self-sufficient depends on my recognizing my own self-sufficient mask and all that really lies behind it. I do that best in solitude.

I used to think that solitude was required as a refueling for myself because I was out there giving so much to others. Now I recognize that I'm out there on stage, playing to the crowds; I need solitude in order to re-discover how needy I really am.

In my moments of solitude words regain their meaning. The "Here, let me show you how that's done" which I spoke on stage, in the dressing room sounds more like "I need to feel important once in awhile, too." My on-stage "I want to serve you" seems in my moments of solitude quite clearly to be, "I need to be needed." And even my "I love you" can sometimes reveal itself in a moment of solitude as "I want to possess you and make you dependent on me." I think I emerge from my moments of solitude more able to use words to *reveal* myself and less tempted to use them to *hide* myself.

The depth of my relationships depends in part on the depth of my self-disclosure. And the depth and accuracy of my self-disclosure depends on the depth and accuracy of my self-awareness. And the depth and accuracy of my self-awareness depends, in turn, on my taking myself seriously enough to enjoy my own company. Solitude and relationships are not opposed to each other; they are interdependent.

Relationships beyond the functional are open to me because I am sexual and I have a need for personal connectedness with others and a capacity for intimacy. But my need does not give me a right to demand that others connect with me. I have a drive to connect in emotional ways with other human beings whom I find attractive and to whom I respond emotionally. But my drives do not give me the right to possess them or make them dependent on me or to become an emotional burden to them. I have genital urges and find myself responding genitally to some people. But my urges do not give me the right to use others for my own gratification. The personal relationships which are open to me because I am sexual and have a personal need for intimacy, emotional drives, and genital urges, are based on appreciation for who another is and on gratitude to the other for what that person gives me because I have need of it.

My needs, drives, and urges impel me toward establishing and maintaining relationships. But it is the *behavior* I choose in making known my needs, drives and urges which will lead to the successful and satisfying establishment of relationships with others or to a frustrated and lonely existence. I am impelled toward fusing with others in genital, emotional and personal ways by my urges, drives and need for intimacy, and I need to direct those impulses with my insight and freedom if the relationships are going to be compatible with who I am and with who the others are. I've noticed that the lasting relationships I've established are based on the mutual appreciation for each other, and the *gratitude* we feel toward each other for what we have done by being ourselves.

Many times I have tried to speak of someone as "my best friend." Each time I have had to correct myself, because as soon as I want to call someone my "best friend" I think of someone else about whom I am inclined to say the same thing. Yet one afternoon I daydreamed at great length about my own dying, and I recognized in the daydream some special relationships I have with four people.

In my daydream I was in the hospital and there were many people around. Lots of faces appeared at my bedside, friends from many years ago and people who are part of my life now. In my daydream I could no longer sustain the effort to welcome all those to whom I wanted to speak before I died. I asked eventually that my visitors be limited to four people: Ron, Jerry, Jan and Paul. I regretted my obvious inability to sustain the conversations with the others, but I simply could not do so.

When I reflected on my daydream, I realized that those four people fill some very important roles in my life. I have with them relationships of special significance. I cannot say they are my "best friends," or single out one as my "best friend," but each seems to epitomize examples of relationships in my life. It is in reflecting on my relationships with them that I have begun to hypothesize about what makes for healthy personal relationships among people.

Ron, who is slightly older than I, was the provincial for whom I served as vicar. He chose me from among four men on his council, which surprised me because we are very different personalities. I had known and thought highly of him since we were in the seminary, and was honored more by his choosing me than by the office itself.

Our relationship began as a functional one. The first time we were alone after the election, we were driving all day back to the office. He said at some point early in the trip, "Keith, I expect that we'll work well together, but I'm a very private person." "That's great!" I said sarcastically; "I'm an exhibitionist!"

Ron explained that he wasn't trying to put me off, "It just takes me awhile to let people know me; I want you to know that. Don't be put off because it takes me awhile."

At first I was a bit concerned, but the self-awareness and self-disclosure Ron exhibited was typical of the way we related to each other for our six years in office. Six years later, when we had finished our terms, I felt free and quite elated about beginning a sabbatical.

Our rooms were next to each other at the place where the chapter was held to elect new provincial officials. I had written Ron a farewell and thank-you note and I gave it to him saying, "Now for the hard part." We gave each other a hug in the corridor and he went into his room and I into mine. Ron returned a few minutes later with the open note in his hand. "Thank you," he said simply. I began to cry and said, ". . . and goodbye."

Two and a half weeks later I was on vacation with four friends at a cottage on a lake. Ron was going to join us the next day. That evening someone mentioned how I seemed to be very relaxed. I assured them that their impression was accurate and that it had not been difficult to forget about what had occupied my thoughts the previous six years. I began to tell them that the only difficult part of leaving office had been saying goodbye to Ron. And I began to cry again.

Through my tears I told my four friends that all my life I had worked in a team situation and all those experiences had been good. But after six months of working with Ron I had written one night in my greenbook that I felt as though I had found my other half. That impression grew and was verified over the six years we worked together.

Ron encouraged and supported what I brought to our relationship, and I supported him. We laughed together several times during our last year in office as we both recognized how much we had rubbed off on each other. Each of us recognized in our last year together that words and phrases which came out of my mouth after five years of association with him were typical of what he would have said five years earlier and vice versa. Because of what rubbed off on me from my "other half" I parted from Ron six years later much more whole.

I cried that night as I told my friends that saying thank you and goodbye to Ron was the most difficult thing I had done. Both Ron and I wanted to leave office. We knew that we would see each other frequently and would make efforts to get together. But our daily being and working together had come to an end for now. I wept, not because I wanted it all to continue as it had been, but because having to say "Thank you" to one from whom I had gained so much and to follow that immediately with "Goodbye" was a deeply painful experience of separation.

It seems so clear to me that our relationship had been given the chance to grow, not because we had similar personalities or because of previous experiences with one another, not because of the functional relationship which brought us together, but because we chose behaviors which had allowed intimacy to arise. Those behaviors were the same ones Ron began that first day in the car: self-awareness and self-disclosure in the hearing of the other. Those behaviors were prompted by the appreciation we had for one another and the gratitude we experienced and expressed for what we did for each other by being ourselves.

The following morning I sat by the lake and reflected on all I had said to my friends. There I recognized a pattern in the special relationships I have with the other three people who are similarly special to me. All of those relationships seem to be based on appreciation for my friends and gratitude to them for what they have given to me by being themselves.

Jerry is a friend I've written about before. When I had first met him as a college student I found him attractive. He was physically good-looking, witty and personable, and very popular with most of his peers and teachers. He was simply a nice guy whom I hoped would grow up happy to be a Capuchin.

He did grow up as a Capuchin and we got to know each other better the year he was a deacon. He initiated several conversations that year, and we allowed each other to know who we were and found we were very different personalities.

Jerry was ordained a priest and assigned to a parish. I saw him seldom. After three years he was asked to go back to school for a degree in psychology. That meant he would be living in an apartment in Chicago with another friar.

One hot August day as I as driving through Chicago, I thought of Jerry and Mark setting up housekeeping in a northside neighborhood. I wanted to get back to Detroit, but I decided to stop for a visit. They were a bit overwhelmed, it seemed to me, at the project they had undertaken. And they seemed to appreciate my visit.

That was only the first of many overnight visits to the house on Hermitage Avenue. During those visits Jerry confided much about his own questions and struggles and his so doing led me to revisit some of my own questions.

I'm ten years older than Jerry, and the times in which I grew up in the Order and as a priest were quite different from the times in which Jerry was growing up. His 1980 questions found no ready answer in my 1970 experience. At some point during the two years Jerry indicated that he could very well leave the Order and the priesthood to pursue a romantic relationship. I was horrified at the thought; I didn't want to lose him. I remember telling him, though, "I won't chase you. But I wish you'd mine me for whatever of my inner experience you might want to know. I don't know if there is anything in here that you can use, but if there is I want you to have access to it." And mine me he did, to his own advantage I hope, and certainly to my benefit.

The conversations we had stand for me as a model of the self-awareness and self-disclosure in the hearing of another which leads to increased self-awareness in the one who hears. Initially finding Jerry attractive prompted me to behave toward him as I did. He let me know him and by doing so invited me to increased self-awareness, which I in turn disclosed to him. Through it all our appreciation for each other and our gratitude toward each other grew. We became friends.

When Jerry finished his studies he was assigned to Detroit, to be on the formation team and to be the local superior of the friary which housed the provincial offices. Ron and I didn't live there, but we worked there. I was happy to be near the man who had become a friend. But our association was quite casual: I'd stop and see him each morning or he'd drop in to my office with his cup of coffee and chat for a few minutes. Almost simultaneously we both felt we were cheating ourselves by the kind of association we were having now that we saw each other almost daily. Our self-disclosure was simply not as significant as it had been when we met infrequently at the Hermitage Avenue apartment.

We decided that we'd make it a point to get together once a month just to talk. We didn't go out to dinner or for a drink, and we never had an agenda. We simply let each other know what was happening in our lives and what we were thinking and feeling. For three or four hours we'd talk and theorize about what concerned us. Much of what I am writing in this book is the result of our monthly get-togethers.

Jerry is the one about whom I am most often inclined to say, "He's my best friend." I can't honestly say that, though, because before I finish the sentence I think of Ron or Paul or Jan or someone else. But I know Jerry knows me because I have allowed him to. With Jerry my self-awareness and my self-disclosure are almost simultaneous. I don't censor what I'm going to tell him about myself. And he listens so well that often my self-awareness increases in my telling him about myself. I have felt at times as though I could walk into his office and say, "Hi, Jerry. How am I?" and he could tell me.

He has given me a great deal because he has been willing to let me know him. And I have come to appreciate him for the person he is. One night we were talking about what had happened to us in our relationship with each other. Jerry became silent for quite a long time and after the pause he said with some dismay, "I *need* Keith Clark." It was for him, he told me, a sobering realization. We talked about that for a long time and together we discovered, we think, something about intimate relationships. The difficulty I had in saying goodbye to Ron is the difficulty I have anticipated for years that I would have when I would have to say goodbye to Jerry. I need Jerry! Period! He's my friend.

I met Jan when she came to the friary for some counselling and spiritual direction. I was instantly fascinated by her. Being in her presence affected me genitally as well as emotionally. I knew almost immediately that this was the woman I'd pursue with marriage in mind if we both hadn't made previous commitments to religious life.

In the course of a couple of years, Jan gradually and steadily decided to leave the religious community in which she was a sister in temporary vows. I wanted her to be a religious, and it was difficult for me to walk with her toward her decision to leave. After she did leave, I still saw her quite frequently because I was close to her whole family. My fascination grew into very strong romantic feelings. I did not tell her at the time my feelings were so strong, because my doing so would have been choosing a behavior that would be a first step toward acting out my romantic inclinations.

We did enjoy each other's company, however, and particularly at gatherings of her family I let her know me and she let me know her. We behaved in ways toward each other which were appropriate to who we were. When I wrote *An Experience of Celibacy*, I showed her the manuscript because she figured so heavily in the experience I wrote about. That was the first time I told her directly of my romantic inclinations toward her. And that was the first time that she told me that she had felt the same way toward me all along!

The romantic feelings we had each harbored for almost 10 years were now spoken. She told me she simply had come to love and respect me too much to do or say anything which would have taken me away from my commitment to religious life. I loved and respected her too much to try to involve her in a romantic relationship which couldn't go anywhere without upsetting a lot of lives. During those years there was no need to speak our feelings directly, because there had been no indirect mixed messages in our behavior which needed explaining. When we did tell each other about our feelings it had quite a different meaning, I suspect, than it would have had we spoken our feelings at the beginning when we could have allowed them to overpower us. Ten years later our speaking could be a statement disclosing our feelings; the behavior we had chosen toward each other those 10 years precluded any mixed messages in our disclosure now.

These past years have seen our love deepen. I knew from the outset that if I would have left my religious commitment and pursued the possibility of marrying Jan, our romantic feelings would find expression in the concrete actions of establishing and maintaining a family. I knew a commitment to Jan in marriage would mature our romantic inclinations for each other into *intimacy* that would find expression in romantic and genital ways. What I didn't know was that love can mature whether or not two people marry.

I am frequently tempted to say, "Jan is my best friend." But I can't. No one is dearer to me, but I always think of others in my life who are as dear in different ways.

I need Jan in my life because of what she has already been for me and done for me. I do not feel indebted to her or obliged to her. I feel free to visit her when I can and free to be away from her. I love her very much.

I've been told by people at workshops that when they read about my relationship with Jan in *An Experience of Celibacy* they thought, "Well, there he goes; he won't be a religious much longer." I appreciate the concern. Her mother has said, as Jan and I have been leaving to do a workshop, "Now, do I have to worry about you two?" to which Jan has responded at times, "Mother, we're only going to *talk* about sex." Recently I was visiting her parent's home, and all the members of the family were leaving to go their different ways. Jan's youngest brother left the room where Jan and I were sitting. Then he returned. "Can I trust you two alone?" he asked with a grin on his face.

I appreciate the realism of such statements; they reflect accurately the romantic inclinations Jan and I feel for each other. I also appreciate the support in such statements for Jan and myself to be true to ourselves in the way we behave toward each other.

Paul is a friend I have known for almost half his 34 years. He was the youngest novice in the first class for whom I served on the novitiate team. I was his teacher and adviser. He was bright and quick to comprehend what I shared of my own theological outlook and my viewpoint on spirituality, and he was creative in formulating a vision of his own. He was the kind of student every first year teacher could hope to have.

I liked Paul and admired him. I also was inclined to try to make myself indispensable in his life. It took a very firm resolution on my part to let go of Paul when he finished his novitiate and moved on to continue his college education and seminary training. I was always happy when I could see him, but over the seven years between his novitiate and his ordination to the priesthood we had little chance to keep up our relationship.

After his ordination Paul and I were both assigned to the novitiate team. Paul was an adult now, and during that year together we related as peers instead of as mentor and student. I learned from him and he learned from me. He let me know him and I let him know me. An intimate relationship grew between us.

I moved from the novitiate team after one year and Paul remained. We kept close contact, deliberately visiting each other, going on vacations together, phoning each other frequently.

One evening Paul was visiting Detroit where I was stationed, and he and Jerry and I were out to dinner. I became sick and all but passed out at the table in the restaurant. The emergency medical service was called, but I revived and Paul and Jerry took me home. It became clear later that my problem in the restaurant was an anxiety attack brought on by over work and a misunderstanding of something Paul and Jerry were saying as we ate our dinner together.

Later that evening as we sorted out the whole incident, I was speaking my mind and heart to Jerry and Paul, neither of whom gave any indication that what I was saying was making any sense to them. Finally I looked at my two friends and said, "Do you understand what I'm saying?" I was almost pleading. Paul said, "Of course I understand; you sired me."

I was in my early forties at that time, that period of life
at which most men would like to be understood by their
sons. Nothing Paul could have said would have pleased me
more. I had tried to behave toward him for over a decade in
such a way that I never claimed him for the son I never had,
and at an age when all sons need to be independent of those
who sired them, Paul acknowledged that in his independence he understood me.

It was a personal desire for a son and my affection for
Paul as the son I would never have which prompted me to
initiate a relationship with him when he was a novice. I
chose to behave toward him in ways which did not simply
gratify those desires, but in ways which allowed intimacy to
arise. I appreciated him and was grateful to him for what he
gave me by being himself. As the years passed, I watched
him grow to adulthood and surpass me in the very things
which I first taught him. As an adult he let me know him,
and I let him know me. I need Paul because of who he is
and what he has already given me by being himself.

I don't know if these are my four best friends. I do
know that my relationships with them are significant to me,
not just because of the love we have for one another, but because these four friends have entered my life in ways which
meet my needs as a human being. The relationships developed in the way they did, not because of my needs, but because of the behavior we all chose. I am a man committed to
a celibate life. That life is fulfilling for me, largely, I suspect,
because in Ron and Jerry and Jan and Paul I have relationships which meet my need to have a mentor, a friend, a
spouse and a son. The behavior through which those relationships were established and maintained allowed them to
arise without our demanding of each other that we be someone other than we have chosen to be. These are deeply personal intimate relationships, and I am very grateful for
them.

It is not my urges and drives or needs which brought

about the intimate relationships I have with these four people; nor is it their appearance or personalities; nor, for that matter, is it the circumstances which brought us into each others' lives. Intimacy could grow *because of the way we behaved* toward each other. The behaviors I chose allowed a personal intimacy to grow instead of merely relationships which would be gratifying to my genital urges and romantic drives or would simply find me filling a role which related to the role which another filled.

I do not mean to be bragging about what I've done; I'm just not willing to abdicate to others, not even to those to whom I am grateful and whom I appreciate deeply, the responsibility for my own happiness. I'm grateful to those who educated me to see things the way I do and to make the kinds of choices of behavior I've made—primarily I guess, to my parents who loved me but still let me go. My behavior alone is not responsible for the intimate relationships which grew; Ron and Jerry, Jan and Paul also chose behaviors which allowed intimacy to grow. I am grateful to them,too.

That's the way it is with personal relationships, I believe. We are motivated to enter them because of functional necessity, genital urges, emotional and romantic drives and a personal need for intimacy. What motivates us is not that which shaped the relationship; the behavior we choose is what allows relationships to develop into personally intimate ones. Those relationships which are intimate are based on appreciation for who the other is and on gratitude for what the other gives to us because of who he or she is. Healthy relationships are not based on indebtedness and a sense of obligation, but on gratitude. Those relationships are allowed to develop because of the self-awareness and self-disclosure and hearing which people choose to do. Or so I have come to believe.

Interlude

What I have written in Part I about being sexual is, in my opinion, true of everyone. I have attempted to express what I have experienced of my own sexuality, and I hope managed to spell out most of my assumptions and ideas about sexuality which underlie my notions about celibate commitment.

For the past 25 years I have experienced being sexual as a man committed to a celibate life. In Part I, I have frequently drawn examples from my own life to illustrate my points about sexuality, and have also drawn on what married and single people have shared with me. In all the examples I meant to illustrate what is true of all of us: We are sexual.

I have dismissed as foolish and even arrogant any attempt on my part to trace the human experience of being sexual down all the paths in which it is lived out. While I have ideas based on what married and single friends have told me of their lives, I have traveled only the path of a celibate commitment within religious life. It is along this path that I feel some comfort in leading others in further reflections on being sexual. I can speak from my own experience of being sexual and celibate.

Our choice in life, be it to a vowed commitment to celibacy in religious life or the priesthood, a vowed commitment to permanence and fidelity in marriage, or being single for any number of reasons, is a choice made for the purpose of loving other human beings. Human fulfillment is found in cherishing and nurturing others even when it costs us something, and whether or not we get something out of it. It is the respectful, non-possessive, non-manipulative, nurturing and accepting of the beloved which makes human fulfillment possible.

In Part Two I want to write about the committed religious life and the experience of being sexual as a celibate man or woman. At least part of the reason celibacy seems so irrelevant to many people is that often there is insufficient recognition of the relationship between the committed celibate life and the whole human experience of intimacy and relationships. As a result, the connection between sexuality and celibacy is almost completely ignored much of the time. People just assume that some people are sexual and others are celibate.

Married life and religious life are often compared and contrasted both in popular thinking and in more formal discussions, usually to the detriment of one or the other lifestyle.

There is great danger for both married and religious people if their lifestyles are seen and thought of primarily in contrast with each other. Religious life can come to be thought of primarily as an un-married life. Married life can be perceived as un-celibate, even mistakenly as un-chaste, denying it the specifically human and Christian basis on which it is built. Statements about the grandeur and beauty—as well as about the difficulty and precariousness—of each way of life seem to diminish the appreciation for the beauty and grandeur, the difficulty and the precariousness of the other. A further difficulty of envisioning these two lifestyles as opposites is the disappearance of any consideration of the single life, except to regard it as the source of candidates for the married or the religious life.

Admitting that there is great danger of misunderstanding inherent in trying to compare married and religious life,

I'm going to attempt to say something about the relationship between them!

People who choose a celibate life are sexual. All of us achieve the meaning of our being sexual by living and loving in such a way that intimacy is possible. To be truly intimate, our coming together must be accomplished in such a way that we don't damage ourselves or the other person; there must be a fusing and a counterpointing of personalities. This counterpointing can occur only if there is a deeply respectful love for oneself and for the beloved. I'm going to borrow a term from Father Adrian van Kaam and call that quality or component necessary for all love to be truly human "respectful distancing." Respectful distancing implies that even in our coming together in the deepest possible intimacy, there is a love which is not imposing and not possessive, a love which is cherishing of the other's being and nurturing of the other's becoming. It implies equally a respectful love for oneself: We do not allow ourselves to be manipulated or dominated or subjugated or in any other way damaged in coming together with another.

This quality of human love is required of all people's loving, no matter what their lifestyle. The celibate attempts to say by the way he or she lives, not merely by words, that human love is about intimacy. The love celibate people have for others is not more respectful than the love spouses have for each other. Celibates adopt as part of their lifestyle the laying aside of romantic pursuits and genital expressions of their love, not because they wish to disparage the romantic and genital aspects of human sexuality, but because doing so is part of their attempt to say by the way they live that all human love has the quality of "respectful distancing."

There is a myth which suggests that when love finds expression in appropriate romantic and genital feelings and behavior it is somehow not nearly so worthy as when expressed in non-romantic and non-genital ways. It is equally a myth that the experience of romantic and genital feelings and behavior indicates the presence of love. An observer cannot tell simply by the presence or absence of romantic and genital feelings and activity whether love for another is present or not. Respectful love for another chooses romantic and genital expression only if it is appropriate to do so, that is, if it can be done without someone being damaged.

All the people who have brought me to consider human sexuality give meaning to my life as a celibate man. My life is intended to say that I have seen the meaning of human loving in the lives of those who love respectfully; it is intended to point out the meaning of human loving in the lives of all those people. Celibates are called to live intensely the personal/spiritual level of sexuality exclusively, remaining unmarried for the sake of their witness to the respectful distancing which makes all human love possible. Of itself, remaining unmarried is neither here nor there; it is by remaining unmarried that celibates attempt to make visible by their lifestyle what all people in all lifestyles are living. My life makes sense to me because the lives of all the others make sense to me.

The absence of romantic and genital behavior from the celibate life does not insure respectful love for others. However the celibate lifestyle still stands as a witness to what is required of all human love, namely, that it be respectful of others.

Love is not like Neapolitan ice cream, which comes in three equal layers of flavors in one carton. It is not as though the more respectful the love the less room there is for genital and romantic feelings and behavior. Nor is it true that the presence of genital and romantic feelings and behavior means love is less respectful. And it is also false to conclude that an absence of romantic and genital feelings implies a more respectful love.

It is simply true that all human love is permeated with a respectful nurturing of the beloved whether or not that love is experienced and expressed in genital and romantic ways.

All this can be said in words, as I have just attempted to do. However, if I say the same thing by the way I live—by organizing my lifestyle exclusively around that quality of human love which is present whether or not I have romantic and genital feelings for another—I show that I do in fact believe in the possibility of respectful loving of human beings. By my lifestyle I hope to help other people believe in the possibility of loving their friends, their spouse, their children, their parents, and yes, even their enemies, in a respectful way. A celibate lifestyle says to those who embrace it and to all others who respect it that human happiness is found in respectful love for each other.

My church accepts marriage as a sacrament, a thing very sacred. When two people commit themselves to each other for life, the believing community accepts what they do as a sign of something we cannot see; namely, the way Christ and his church are committed to each other. I cannot see how fully Christ has accepted us. But I can see two people commit themselves to each other in marriage. Marriage is a sacrament, a sign which points to a reality I cannot see.

A celibate commitment is not a sacrament; it points to something which can be seen but which might be overlooked; namely, that true human love has the quality of respectful distancing. I have chosen a celibate lifestyle because the lives of so many others with other lifestyles make sense to me. My commitment means that I will remain unmarried, that I will not have a family and children of my own. I will remain unmarried as a way of showing by the way I live that the lives of all people have meaning because of their respectful and nurturing love for one another.

If the public celibate commitment of the religious life is accompanied by romantic or genital behavior, it is not celibacy. If remaining unmarried is accompanied by manipulative and possessive behavior and attitudes, it is not celibacy. If remaining unmarried is thought to be a heroic privation and is compensated for by self-indulgence, it is not celibacy. Religious life means a lot more than remaining unmarried. It means a lot more than refraining from genital and romantic pursuits. Celibacy includes the personal and spiritual aspects of being sexual. It is affectionate, warm, emotional. Sometimes a celibate is *affected* romantically and genitally by the relationships he or she has with others, but romance and genital *activity* are not pursued.

Behavior externalizes what goes on inside people; it is public; it has consequences, both personal and social. Marriage and religious life are different in their demands and possibilities because of the behaviors which comprise each lifestyle and the consequences of those behaviors. They are not different because celibates experience a different kind of intimacy than married people do. They don't. But the behaviors through which intimacy is expressed are different. The "I need you" of an intimate conjugal relationship is not different from the "I need you" of an intimate celibate relationship. When the intimacy is expressed genitally, however, the consequences are significantly different. By the nature of their commitment to each other in marriage and the genital expression they give to their intimacy, spouses promise that they will be there for each other in the future. Their lifestyle is formed by their commitment and the behaviors by which they express their intimacy. Spouses can't separate without detriment to each other and to their commitment. Celibates can separate from those with whom they have intimate relationship. The difference is not in the intimacy but in the lifestyle they have chosen to pursue.

Each lifestyle places unique demands on those who commit themselves to it. The unique demands of religious life do not dictate what a celibate feels and experiences but they do determine the behaviors we can choose and the kind of relationships we can form as a result of those behaviors.

There are many things which can be said about a commitment to a celibate life beyond those which have to do with sexuality. I attempted to say some of those things in *An Experience of Celibacy*. Others have said beautifully other things about the religious life. In Part Two I will focus only on things which are true of the celibate precisely because he or she is also sexual.

Since *An Experience of Celibacy* was published, I have been involved in many discussions. Very few of those discussions have revolved around the nature of celibacy. Most have been about understanding sexuality; and many of those were based on the assumption that celibacy would be easier to live and to understand if those who chose that way of life weren't also sexual. Being celibate doesn't seem to be difficult to understand; neither does being sexual. But being sexual and celibate poses a great many questions for many people. And the questions are usually not speculative for those who raise them. The questions are usually raised at a point of conflict between a celibate commitment and a growing desire to pursue a romantic relationship. If a person waits to examine his or her experience until this point, either sexuality or celibacy will seem unfriendly—celibacy an unfriendly captor or sexuality an unfriendly intruder. The conclusion that one or the other is unfriendly is the first step toward leaving a celibate commitment.

I am grateful to those who have invited me to accompany them on their journey out of religious life. They have shared their experiences and the stories they have told themselves about their experiences. Often I have disagreed with the stories to some degree. Others have shared their thinking and their questions as they moved toward making a life commitment to celibacy; they too have been my teachers. Frequently those who were sorting out their lives invited me to tell them how I interpreted their experiences. Their invitation has been the impetus for my clarifying for myself what I think about being sexual and celibate.

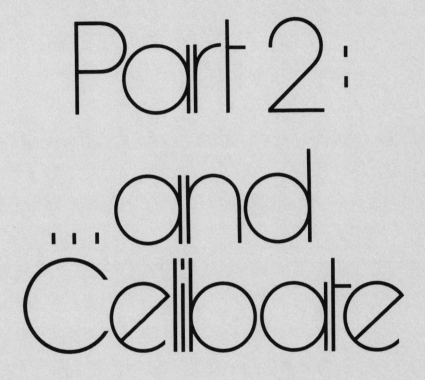

Part 2:
...and
Celibate

Chapter 7
Hidden and Forbidden

When I was still very young—before I began high school—I experienced erections which were sometimes accompanied by a secretion of a drop of clear liquid. I knew one of the neighbor boys had had an operation of some kind because there was something wrong with his appendix. I just knew something was wrong with my appendix too, and that was the reason for my leaking the clear liquid from my penis. Of course I never told anyone what I experienced or the way I understood it. They would all find out soon enough when I was rushed to the hospital for my appendix operation!

It all sounds rather ludicrous to me now, but at eleven years old I was confronted with something about being sexual which was obvious but which was also mysterious and needed an explanation. There were people around who could have explained, but I knew that you just didn't ask questions about being sexual. With the grown-ups you pretended nothing was happening and with the other kids you pretended you knew all about what was happening.

As silly as it sounds, I know that I and a lot of other people many times the age I was when I had the "problem with my appendix" have continued to grasp at facile explanations for what is obvious but mysterious about being sexual rather than talk about it with someone who is better informed.

I remain grateful to the newer and usually younger members of my Order, for whom I served as novice director. They were daring and trusting enough to share some of their questions with me. Though seldom formulated directly, their most frequent question was, "Am I normal in what I am experiencing and realistic in what I am planning—namely, to pursue a celibate vocation—since I am experiencing being sexual?"

I'm not sure what they gained in those talks we had about being sexual and celibate, but I gained a sense that I was normal! I also gained confidence in a steadily growing belief that my sexuality is friendly and I can trust it. My sexuality didn't become more friendly because I told others about what I experienced, but I began to recognize that it had been friendly all along. I have also learned that I cannot befriend my sexuality alone; I need the help of another with whom I can talk freely.

The benefit of talking about the experience of being sexual is greatest for those who can recognize and speak about the biological level of having a body, the bio-psychological level of emotions and attractions and the personal/spiritual level of our need for intimacy.

I remember several significant events in childhood which had to do with becoming comfortable with my body, but most of them are too distantly connected to my adult experience of being sexual to recount. I was tall; that was a plus, except when the woman at the ticket window of the local movie theater wanted me to pay adult admission because she wouldn't believe that I was only eleven. My feet were big; that was a minus. My chin was small; that was a minus, especially when my best friend and his younger brother had finely chiseled features.

With the beginning of puberty I experienced a lot of physical arousal. I became afraid of the shower room at the gym and the pool, because it would be so embarrassing if I had an erection in front of the other boys. The fact that I never did get an erection didn't lessen the fear much.

I learned the word "masturbation" when I went to high school and I was taught it was bad, though I was never led to believe it had the horrible consequences some other boys were told it had. But I connected the word and its implications to the embarrassingly obvious yet mysterious experience of frequent erections. I was blessed with the friendship of a priest at the high school seminary with whom I could talk. When I told him about getting aroused sexually, his whole demeanor as well as his words helped me know I was normal and it might be realistic for me to continue my pursuit of a way of life which included a commitment to celibacy.

Growing up I never had the occasion to go skinny dipping, but it always seemed like it would be a marvelous experience. At age 29 I was assigned to our novitiate team. The friary had a pool secluded enough from view that swimming suits were frequently laid on the edge immediately after the novices dove in.

I don't enjoy swimming very much but on hot, muggy Indiana nights the thought of a plunge was very inviting. And the prospect of skinny-dipping only added to the enticement. But with the enticement came the old shower-room fear of having an erection and of being embarrassed in front of the whole group of novices.

On different occasions novices told me of their fear of joining in the fun lest they get an erection. At first I played it real cool and never let on that I had the same desire and fear. Eventually I got the courage to tell one novice, "Yeah, I know what you mean; I'm the same way."

As others spoke haltingly of their experience, I got the impression that I was not alone in the world of reluctant skinny-dippers. And I saw relief on the faces of those with whom I shared my desire and my fear of swimming naked.

Skinny-dipping is a preference, not a virtue. There is no reason why anyone *ought to* do it. On the other hand, in the proper setting there was no reason not to do it.

I watched people handle their discomfort and have generalized that there are three ways people deal with it in regard to their bodies. Some *pretended* that they were comfortable with what they wanted to do and went ahead and did it. Some novices just pretended they were perfectly comfortable slipping off their swimming suit in the pool. They convinced themselves that what they wanted to do was OK, and pretended they felt OK about doing it.

Others thought it was OK, but admitted that they didn't feel OK about doing it. So they always wore their swimming suits. They decided just to wait until they felt comfortable before they did it.

And some of the novices tried a third way. They talked to me and to a classmate or two about their desire and their fear even though they saw nothing wrong with it. *Admitting they were uncomfortable, they decided to do it* anyway, not because it was necessary, but just because it was OK and they wanted to.

I noticed that those who decided to wait until they felt comfortable never reached that point. Those who pretended they were comfortable didn't seem to become comfortable with the activity. The only group which seemed to move from discomfort to comfort was the group which admitted feeling uncomfortable with doing something they considered OK and decided to do it because it was OK.

Now, that's a long story for the small, but I think, important point. A person does not *have to* feel comfortable with and do everything some other people are at ease with. But there seems to be only one way to become comfortable with an uncomfortable bodily aspect of sexuality; rationally ascertain the legitimacy of the activity, admit the desire and the fear of the activity and then choose to act, not out of some compulsion and not pretending to be comfortable with what you are not.

Skinny-dipping is just one activity to which this approach applies. Some other activities are talking about sex, sleeping naked, looking at your body in a mirror, being naked in the presence of others, touching your body, being touched, hugging, kissing and other expressions of affection. There is no compelling reason to perform them; there is no reason, in many instances, for not performing them. Those who decide not to perform them because of their discomfort make a good decision, I think. Those who decide to go ahead and do what they have decided is OK even though they feel uncomfortable also make a good decision, because the activity is OK. Those who pretend to be comfortable make a bad decision, one which does not lead to comfort no matter how often the activity is repeated.

Beyond the simple fact that celibate people have bodies just like everyone else, there are hosts of other aspects of sexuality which are frequently obvious but mysterious and which are related to our bio-psychological level. The column and the reservoir seem filled with irrational and impulsive fantasies, urges, attractions, curiosities and sexual emotions. For people who are committed to a celibate life or considering one, the opportunity to explore romantically the irrational and impulsive aspects of sexuality is not there. But the drive toward romantic and genital activity remains.

Since romantic activity usually suggests the possibility of choosing each other as mates, it is not appropriate to those considering or committed to a celibate life. It does seem appropriate that they are at least aware enough of other possibilities that they are making a choice from a variety of good options.

By that I do not mean to imply that people who are thinking about being religious or priests ought to do some romancing prior to entering a seminary or a pre-novitiate program; that would just be using someone for self-exploration. But seminarians and candidates for religious life ought to know at least that they could pursue other ways of life.

I had thought that the difference in the experiences

people had prior to entering the seminary or the novitiate would mean that there would be a different degree of comfort people felt with their columns and reservoirs. I welcomed the requirement that a candidate for our novitiate be the equivalent of at least a college junior before he could be accepted. In fact, most of those who applied for novitiate had been out of high school for four years. I felt sure that increased life experience would reduce the number of issues concerning sexuality which people would have to deal with during their years of initial formation.

I remember that I felt a little inadequate and intimidated as I faced for the first time the prospect of a novitiate class comprised mostly of college graduates. I had entered novitiate after one year of college and had never dated seriously. I figured the incoming novices would be much more sophisticated in sexual matters than I had been at their age and, perhaps, more knowledgeable than I was at the time I was teaching them. I presumed that they had answered for themselves questions for which I was simply lacking the evidence to answer definitively.

Time and a lot of listening corrected those assumptions. Those who had dated and even been engaged, harbored the same questions as those who had not: Am I normal and am I realistic in pursuing a celibate life, granted what I know of my sexual urges and drives and needs?

I am not reporting the results of a scientific survey. I want merely to present what I have come to know and to think as a result of the listening I have done to my own and to others' experience.

Most of us, with few exceptions, grew up in an atmosphere in which sexual matters were spoken of infrequently. We experienced our own sexuality as obvious but mysterious. It presented a lot of unknowns. Our curiosity about most things was encouraged, but not in sexual matters. What was unknown frequently seemed also hidden. That increases curiosity, I'm convinced, but it bars us from approaching openly those who could satisfy our curiosity with some accuracy. For many, sexuality was not only something unknown and hidden, it also took on the aura of the forbidden. The territory seemed strewn with a myriad of "don'ts." That can increase normal sexual curiosity to the level of an obsession.

Some of those to whom I've listened seem to almost relish the chance to blame their parents and early teachers for their fear of exploring their own experience of being sexual. Seminary profs and religious formation personnel are other scapegoats for people's present unwillingness to deal with their experience of being sexual. I figure parents had parents too, and seminary profs had seminary profs, and formation directors and directoresses were in initial formation at one time too. The process of blaming predecessors can go on endlessly; and Adam and Eve cannot possibly be held accountable for *all* my present behavior!

One evening I was a dinner guest with two married couples and four children. After dinner the kids went into the living room while the adults lingered long over dessert and coffee. The hostess was seated in the chair nearest the living room where a hushed and serious conversation was taking place among the children. She smiled a few times and made comment about snatches of the children's conversation. The conversation was about sex.

Later I was in the kitchen with the hostess when her 6-year-old approached her, obviously wanting a private word. As I hung up my dishtowel I overheard the boy say that he had learned in the children's conversation that beer helped couples with love-making. His mother said, "No, that's not right; beer isn't necessary at all." Her son went back to his play. His mother chuckled and said that the same son at two and a half years asked his father why his penis got hard and warm sometimes. His dad answered, "That's just the way it is with us boys sometimes."

Few of us, I suspect, grew up in such an open atmosphere. I presume that for those children, when sexual questions arise, their natural curiosity about the unknown will be satisfied with accurate information. For them it won't become the hidden or the forbidden.

Those of us who did not grow up in that kind of environment should not use that fact as an excuse for not imitating that 6-year-old now. We may not have been encouraged to do so when we were children or in the seminary or in initial religious formation, but we can choose to speak about our experience and to examine the stories we tell ourselves. What is unknown need not remain for us hidden and forbidden.

I have been led to this viewpoint, because many novices and younger religious, along with some very close friends, have been trusting and daring enough to raise with me their own questions about their experience of being sexual. They have given me the courage to explore the meaning of what was for me obvious but mysterious and to examine the stories I told myself. Many a novice left my office more comfortable about his experience of being sexual than I was about mine. The difference was that they had talked with someone they trusted; I had not.

I entered religious life with assumptions about my sexuality. I didn't examine those assumptions at the time; I was not even aware of most of them. Because I had spoken about my high school and early college experience of being sexual with a priest I trusted and was reassured that entering religious life was a realistic possibility for me, I assumed that sexuality would not be a very important issue in my life from novitiate on. And it wasn't, largely because those things I experienced and talked about in my early twenties were rarely dealt with as sexual issues by those in whom I confided. Impure thoughts which caused physical arousal were my only sexual issue for years, as far as I knew.

I recognize now that the affection and attraction I felt for my peers were sexual issues because they were experiences of my bio-psychological drives. The lasting friendships

which I formed and which continue to this day were part of
my meeting my need for intimacy. My attraction to and appreciation for the families of my fellow students were an experience of my desire to have a family of my own. When I
experienced a greater interest in the sister of a fellow student
than in the rest of his family, I dismissed it as unworthy and
simply behaved awkwardly toward her when she was
around.

None of these experiences of being sexual became problems for me except a particular friendship I had with a classmate. I found him attractive and liked being with him. I
talked with my directors about it, and I was given the an-
cient and sage advice about not behaving toward him any
differently than I did toward my other friends. I followed
the advice, but I did not consciously relate the whole experience to questions of sexual orientation.

During those years I hid my experience of being sexual
from myself, from others and from God. I broke off my impure thoughts when they got too enticing and I dealt with
my affection for my particular friend as a matter of charity
and community life, not as a matter of sexuality. I was
happy then, and I don't think I have experienced any damage as a result of dealing with my sexuality as I did.

Our view of sexuality becomes distorted if the only impression we have is that sex is enticing and forbidden; sex is
more than that. Sexual behavior has consequences. Ironic as
it seems, impure thoughts are impure because they are *not*
about sex as sex really is.

In workshops I have given with Jan and Jerry, we sometimes asked the participants to examine their most enticing
or most frequently reoccurring pleasant sexual fantasy. We
invite them to follow that fantasy through to its realistic
imagined consequences. If you acted out your sexual fantasy,
what would it be like for you an hour later, or a day later, or
a year later? The realization people often come to is that
their fantasies may be pleasant at the point at which they

are most enticing, but they are disappointing often in their consequences.

If I acted out my sexual fantasy, for instance, the nature of many of the relationships in my life would be considerably different, and I don't want them to be different. If I gratified my sexual urges and drives as I fantasize about doing, I would become quite a different person because doing so would destroy the commitment I have made to a celibate life. These impure thoughts of mine are not about sex as sex really is, because they don't include the consequences of sexual behavior.

I have also decided that I don't want to deal with the experiences of my bio-psychological drives by hiding from myself the fact that my column is full of irrational and impulsive urges and drives, fears and fantasies, and ambiguities. When I relegate these aspects of myself to the realm of the forbidden, like impure thoughts, they become more enticing because they are never checked out for their realism. I've decided that I want to know the content of my column because only then can I choose freely to behave in ways compatible with the celibate commitment I have made.

I don't expect that I'll ever know the content of my column definitively, because it seems as though I continue to be surprised by what it reveals. But I like to keep current on what's going on inside of me, so I pay attention to my biological urges, my bio-psychological drives and my need for intimacy as I experience them.

I have found that this kind of awareness has reduced the number of things which have genital significance for me. There was a day when any kind of hugging or kissing, touch or verbal expression of affection had genital implications for me. I avoided them because they seemed forbidden to one who had a celibate commitment. But relegating them to the realm of the forbidden seems to increase their genital and romantic significance considerably. If people do not allow themselves to experience their bodies and if they hold back from words and physical expressions of affection which are socially appropriate, it seems that these take on an erotic significance they don't necessarily have.

Today the most pressing question about the bio-psychological level of sexuality for a lot of people, including some priests and religious, is that of sexual orientation. Celibate men and women frequently harbor doubts about their primary sexual orientation. Many tell themselves that they lack the necessary evidence to reach a definitive conclusion as long as they refrain from acting out their sexuality genitally or romantically. They presume that a romantic affair or intercourse with a person of the other sex would forever lay the question to rest. It wouldn't.

When I grew up in religious life, the general population didn't talk about homosexuality with the same freedom as most people do today, and certainly not with the care and understanding with which many people do now. It was a hidden and forbidden area, so any experience of attraction to another person of the same sex was destined to remain mysterious. Curiosity about that subject—and talking about it—was stifled completely and facile and more acceptable understandings brought forward. Emotional attractions to other members of the community may have been highly suspect by those in charge, but most often individuals were dealt with on the issue by a quite formal silence or general warnings about such activities. The hidden and forbidden atmosphere which surrounded any same-sex feelings most likely increased the enticement of the feelings, and for some may have led to a kind of obsession which blocked out any recognition of other-sex feelings which a person may have had.

That very indirect approach to the question is lamentable. But it was reflective of the inadequate appreciation of the role of sexuality in human life which was prevalent in the general population. Not exploring what was obvious but mysterious about bio-psychological drives is a mistake; but the advice which people got about concentrating their attention on the behavior they chose in response to those drives was a good one, I think.

From the late 60s until the mid-70s, homosexuality became much more public and took on political significance. Gradually it became all but unacceptable to live with any ambiguity about our dominant sexual orientation. We had to declare ourselves, as the pressure to "come out" mounted. Those who discovered that they not only had sexual feelings for another person of the same sex, but who were also told that they were attractive to another man or to another woman, seemed more quickly to end the ambiguity by deciding they were gay.

Once the decision was made the anxiety of the ambiguity abated. Some sought counselling to aid themselves in their acceptance of the identity they had assumed. They sought and found support from others who had come through the same struggle of self-understanding and self-acceptance. "That question" answered at last, they took up the other tasks of life.

Some others left religious life or the active ordained ministry and became romantically or genitally active. Some remained in religious communities and in the active ordained ministry and permitted themselves occasional or regular romantic and genital forays. They were no longer seeking conclusive evidence to answer the question of their dominant sexual orientation, but regarding celibacy as a marital status only, they thought it inevitable that they find some way to act out their sexuality while remaining unmarried.

I have been personally affected by the cultural changes which have taken place in ways of addressing the issue of homosexuality and by the listening I have done to men and women religious and to priests who have invited me to accompany them on their self-exploration. I have formed some opinions on the matter, but those I'll save for later. For now, something more personal.

One night while I was sitting alone in my room in a retreat house where I was taking part in a meeting at which a
portion of the agenda was homosexuality I decided I was
"gay." I had read a lot on the subject, and I had attended
meetings and workshops where the issue was discussed. I
was doing my nightly writing in my greenbook when I was
overtaken by the sense that I was predominantly homosexual. I became instantly depressed and embarrassed to recognize how prejudiced I was against "them."

I sat in my room for about an hour before I went to the
room of a friend and told him what I had just experienced.
All he did was listen.

The next afternoon the meeting ended and I drove
home with my friend. "How are you feeling?" he asked.
"Still depressed," I said. That day and for the next several
days I just lived with my new realization. In my mind I reviewed my past; my childhood friends, the almost exclusively
male environment of the high school seminary and initial religious formation days, the fact that most of my closest
friends were men. I recalled the emotional fascination I had
had with my "particular friend" during my early years in
the Order. The lack of romantic and genital experience with
any woman before or after I entered the Order raised doubts
that I would have become romantically involved had I not
entered the Order. The only people in whose presence I had
ever been naked were men, and that had always brought
with it the fear of sexual arousal. All of this, I could see, was
evidence that I was gay.

I talked about all this with my spiritual director. And I
went about the tasks my life presented a little more subdued
than usual. About two weeks after my initial realization that
I was gay, I was once again with the friend in whom I had
first confided. He said, "You look as though you're doing
pretty well."

In fact I was doing very well. I had in those two weeks
come full circle. After my initial overwhelming impression
had hit me, I reviewed my life for evidence supportive of

what I had decided. It was clearly there. As I laid the issue aside to take up the rest of my life, however, it became equally evident that I had to ignore a lot of the data of my life in order to arrive at the conclusion that I was gay. There was no way I could make the label stick.

I'm not sure what came over me in that room at the retreat house; but I hypothesize that because of my involvement with quite a few people who were sorting out their own sexual orientation, the workshops I had attended and the reading I had done, I focused my attention almost exclusively on sources of information *outside of my own experience*. There were some similarities, I knew, between what others experienced in their bio-psychological level and what I knew to be true in my own experience. Because I attributed significant authority to those whose opinions I had come to respect, without at the same time seriously examining my own experience, I became for a while divorced from what I knew for sure because I had experienced it.

What is significant to me about the whole experience now is that I examined again what was obvious but mysterious in my column. I had too facilely assigned a meaning to what I found there when I concluded I was gay. I had talked to friends who really knew me and whom I trusted about what I had found. They offered no interpretation and they didn't argue with the one I had given. They provided me with the chance to explore the irrational and impulsive side of my sexuality. And that was helpful. I learned something from it all: it is not helpful to allow others to tell me what my experience is or what it means.

The advantage to celibate people is great if they are comfortable with their bodies and cognizant of the biological aspects of their sexuality. Knowing the content of our column or reservoir as well as the other aspects of the bio-psychological level is also advantageous. Most important, however, is for priests and religious to acknowledge and own the need for intimacy and that they create strategies to have that need met within their celibate lifestyle.

Many of us priests and religious do not recognize and do not deal well with intimacy. I am convinced that that failure is responsible for a lot of the pain and frustration we experience while we try to live out our celibate commitment faithfully. Failure to recognize and deal with the issue of intimacy has caused many priests and religious to leave their communities or the active ordained ministry. Some fear the very word "intimacy" and belittle its use. Others believe they are above such issues and simply ignore or deny that they have any need for intimacy. Still others don't expect that their lives in community and ordained ministry are a possible source of intimacy and they neglect those ways of behaving which could allow intimacy to arise. And some deal well with their own need for intimacy. Through their skill at self-awareness, self-disclosure and hearing they have invited many others to behave in ways which have been good for us as human beings who are called to a celibate life.

The biological aspects of being sexual may seem mysterious, but they are undeniably obvious most of the time. The bio-psychological aspects are difficult to ignore unless we simply refuse to focus our attention on them when they reveal themselves. The personal/spiritual aspects of human sexuality are much less obvious, due partly to the fact that they can be recognized only by insight, and partly because they are all but ignored within our culture. But the need for intimacy is real for everybody, for celibate people as well as for all other human beings.

Our biological *urges* reveal themselves in our bodies. Our bio-psychological *drives* reveal themselves in our emotions. Our personal/spiritual *need* for intimacy reveals itself most clearly when it is being abundantly met or when it is not being met at all. In either case it can go unrecognized as our need for intimacy which is being met or frustrated, because it is not felt directly in our bodies or in our emotions.

About nine years ago, after I was given a job that demanded a lot of travel, I said to a friend, "I think my body gets lonely for a familiar place just the way the rest of me gets lonely when I'm gone from home too long." I was hypothesizing on the experience of becoming increasingly sexually responsive in a physical sense the longer I was on the road. "You mean you get horny when you're gone too long?" he asked, putting the matter into the vernacular. But the simple fact was that I felt more "horny." I felt greater physical and emotional urges and drives toward genital and romantic behavior when I was away from home for a longer time.

Over the past nine years I have begun to tell myself a different story. It isn't that my body knows a loneliness of its own. I now think that because my biological urges and my bio-psychological drives are given to me as an impetus toward establishing and maintaining intimate relationships with others, those urges and drives become more glamorous when I do not choose behavior which allows me to meet my need for intimacy. When my need for intimacy is not being met because I am not engaging in sufficient self-awareness and self-disclosure in the hearing of others, I am more inclined to act out in genital and romantic ways. I "fall in love" with stewardesses on my way home after a couple of weeks of travel much more often than in other circumstances.

I don't believe that simply gratifying my urge for physical sex or my drive for romantic involvement will ever satisfy my human need for intimacy. But if I ignore or deny my need for intimacy, I can expect those aspects of myself which are more instinctual to push me with more than usual force. If my biological urge and my bio-psychological drive are simply indulged and gratified in themselves, the activities only become addictive, while the underlying hunger for intimacy remains unmet. For as long as I allow my need for personal intimacy to remain unmet, I can expect to experience a heightened urgency in my desire for genital sex and romantic involvement.

Celibate people who do not acknowledge and own their need for intimacy and who therefore do not behave in ways which will allow intimacy to arise and be nourished in their lives can expect that sexuality will become a problem for them. It is not their celibate commitment which gives them the problem, it is their refusal to admit and to deal with their need for intimacy which is causing the difficulty. If they were to leave religious life to engage in romantic and genital behavior which did not promote personal intimacy, they would experience the same frustration.

Jerry argued his point that "Human sexuality is about intimacy, period!" a long time ago. I wouldn't be convinced then; now I am convinced. As celibate people we are as sexual as anybody else, and that means our need for intimacy is like everybody else's.

Just because the lifestyle we have chosen does not admit of genital and romantic behavior as expressions of intimacy that does not mean that we can ignore or deny our need for intimacy without detriment to ourselves. If our need for intimacy is ignored or denied, we will need to repress our biological urges and bio-psychological drives as well. And if we engage in that kind of repression, we become time bombs waiting to explode. We may live out our lives before the explosion occurs, but the life we lead will be depleted by our abiding fear of human contact. We will reinforce in our own minds as well as in the perception of others that some people are sexual and others are celibate. If at some point the urgency of our urges and drives bursts into consciousness, we will be convinced that since we now know we are sexual, we can no longer live a celibate life.

My own experience has convinced me that acknowledging and owning our sexuality makes a celibate life possible. Acknowledging is not enough, because one who recognizes

his or her biological urges and bio-psychological drives can
be led to believe that he or she "must be true to myself" and
be convinced that he or she has to act out the urge for genital sex and the drive toward romantic involvements. We need
to go beyond acknowledging our sexuality to the point of
owning or accepting what is true of us. Then we can choose
the behaviors which will allow our need for intimacy to be
met in our relationships to God and to other people within a
celibate lifestyle.

Celibate people *are* sexual. Human sexuality *is* about
intimacy. The least likely candidate for a celibate life is one
for whom sexuality is hidden and forbidden. The most likely
candidate is the one who acknowledges and owns his or her
sexuality in all its aspects—biological, bio-psychological and
personal/spiritual—and can talk about it.

Newer members of religious communities or of the seminary community will be hard pressed to seek out someone
they can trust in the matters of sexuality if among the vet-
erans there is little recognition of the benefit in doing so.
Most of us could learn a lot from the example of a 6-year-old
boy who asked his parents about those things having to do
with sexuality which became obvious to him but which were
mysterious.

Chapter 8
Labels and Judgments

I can trust my column or reservoir for no reason other than that it is me. I can trust it enough to recognize, acknowledge, explore and own what I find there. But it's obvious that I find it difficult to just claim as my own much of the irrational and impulsive side of my experience of being sexual.

Much of my difficulty in acknowledging and owning the irrational and impulsive side of my sexuality arises because the meaning of what I find is more often than not preempted by others. People have already made judgments about the meaning of some of what's in my column or reservoir.

Labels are generalizations imposed on me which lump me with everyone else who has the same label. That inspires in me a certain hesitance to reveal who I am sexually, because I may lose my individuality.

The labels and judgments about sexuality exist in my own mind as well. In an effort to preserve my unique identity I'm often reluctant to acknowledge to myself what's in my column or reservoir, let alone reveal it to someone else.

This is a two-edged sword, however. I may ignore or deny who I am in order to save myself the generalization of the label or judgment, but I lose myself because secretly I harbor a fear of who I am. I fail to own myself because I assume I am the only one among my acquaintances who finds within me those particular irrational and impulsive urges and drives. I end up feeling isolated or alienated from even my circle of friends, because I wonder if they'd still be my friends "if they knew."

By now I've come to assume that my friends are just like me. They have their own set of irrational and impulsive urges and drives, their own set of fears, doubts, wonderings and misgivings. I presume they too wonder sometimes if I'd be their friend "if I only knew."

The therapeutic process, whether done professionally or in the ordinary give and take of friendship, consists of exploring our column or reservoir and sharing what is found there without being labelled or judged. There is an extreme on either side of this therapeutic approach. On one extreme is my and others' pat generalizations of me and my experience; on the other extreme is the isolation of unexamined, unexplored and unshared data.

Between these two extremes lies the possibility of an appropriate intimacy brought about by mutual transparency between friends.But that doesn't happen very often because the labels and judgments about sexual matters loom so large in most of our perceptions.

Labels can be helpful because they provide a way of communicating information. But they can be treacherous if they are used to try to communicate *who I am*. In that, they're a lot like the titles which go with an office or the name given to a role or function. The titles and the names do not communicate the person; they seem to submerge the person beneath the expectations of the role or office.

I remember an experience I had when my first book was published. I had never met an author except when one was giving a lecture where I was one of hundreds of people in the audience. The day that the first copies of *Make Space, Make Symbols* (Ave Maria Press, 1979) were delivered to my office, our auditors were going over the Provincial's finances and several of them asked me for copies of the book. And they wanted them autographed! I just didn't know how to wear the "author" hat gracefully.

Labels just don't communicate very well who someone is; they're all right for communicating information about what someone does or the office someone holds or some aspect of personality or behavior.

This is nowhere more true than in the area of human sexuality, because sexual labels have been very politicized. If I explore what I find in my column or reservoir, and if I know there are labels for what I find there, the only honest thing to do may seem to be to accept the label. In some ways this can be true. But in other ways the label can create realities which otherwise would not be there.

The most politicized sexual labels today are those which have to do with sexual orientation: homosexual, heterosexual, "gay," "straight." I am concerned about the use of the labels and the judgments they imply.

My contention is that the heavy reliance on labels describing sexual orientation makes it difficult to understand what we're talking about. The labels are so highly politicized that I'm afraid many could not hear what I want to say if I used those labels to illustrate what I want to say. So I'll use "heterosexual" and "straight" to illustrate my point. I think the same point applies also to "homosexual" and "gay."

If I have accepted for myself the label heterosexual or straight, I'm happy to do so. I respond emotionally to the label, not just to what I discover in my column or reservoir, and it is politically acceptable in our society to wear this label. Besides the emotional response there is an invitation to distort my perception of myself and others because I have accepted the label heterosexual or straight.

There is a distortion of my perception of others because my acceptance invites me to see all others as either "us" or "them." I may not know whether an individual person is an us or a them, but I figure he or she is one or the other. My speaking with and listening to that person will be influenced by my knowledge that he or she is an us or a them, or by my lack of knowledge about which one a person is. The politicization of the labels leads me to raise questions about another's sexual orientation long before our experience of being sexual becomes a topic of our conversation.

I was driving once with a man who identified himself as being predominantly same-sex oriented. He was the editor of a newsletter which was sent to a group of homosexually oriented men. I asked if I could be put on his mailing list. He said, "No, I can't do that, because the articles are signed and some of our members wouldn't want anyone but another gay to know their identity." For him, I was clearly a them although I had never discussed my dominant sexual orientation with him.

The distortion of perception of others can at times be painfully embarrassing, as it was for me one evening standing at a bus stop with two of my acquaintances who did not know each other. One of them identifies himself as predominantly same-sex oriented. The other acquaintance introduced into our conversation the topic of "those gays," and he continued to speak in a sweeping and casually condemning way of "them," presuming, no doubt, that he was speaking to two of "us." His perception was distorted, and I was embarrassed for him.

My perception of myself can also be distorted because of my having accepted a politicized label. What urges, feelings, drives, and other aspects of my bio-psychological level I find in my column or reservoir will almost certainly be influenced by the label I accept. If I accept the label heterosexual or straight, I am much less likely to attend to any feelings, urges, drives, fantasies, etc., I experience which might contradict or not be compatible with the label I have accepted.

Besides creating an emotional response to the label and the possible distortion of perception, there is in accepting a politicized label the danger of *establishing and meeting ex-*

pectations implied by the label. These expectations are about my behavior and even my interior experience. If I am heterosexual I set expectations about how I will and will not respond emotionally to men and women. I will be drawn toward responding emotionally and behaviorally in ways expected of straights.

I have used the labels heterosexual and straight to illustrate my point, because the politicization of the labels "homosexual" and "gay" is so great that many of us cannot get beyond the label to see any point at all. Accepting the label homosexual or gay has inherent in it the same dangers, though highly intensified. The emotional response, the distortion of perception of oneself and of others and the laying of expectations we are subtly induced to meet vary with individuals. But I do not think the labels are neutral for anybody any more.

Once my perception of myself and others is distorted and once expectations have been laid, my behavior is greatly influenced. I may be inclined to associate more or almost exclusively with us and to avoid and feel awkward among them. I may feel that I ought to, out of some kind of loyalty, associate only or generally with us and not too frequently or at all with them. The distortion of my perception and the laying of expectations may further suggest how I associate with us and how I associate with them in order that I not be confused with them.

It may seem—and may actually be—honest to accept a label. But it needs to be done with awareness that because labels are politicized they do more than name reality and communicate information; they tend to create realities. I think it would be wise to accept and use the labels homosexual and heterosexual only as adjectives and not as nouns. I have tried to strike from my way of speaking such statements as "they are gays" and "they are straights."

Limiting ourselves to the use of the terms as adjectives

makes speaking and communicating more cumbersome, but I think it also makes it more accurate. I prefer not to apply sexual labels to someone's person.

Any attempt I make to identify my self with, or to seek happiness and personal meaning at the biological or bio-psychological level will lead only to frustration and disappointment. If I identify myself as male and seek fulfillment either in marriage or in a celibate life on the basis of that biological reality, I will be frustrated and disappointed.

I am indeed a male. But if that becomes solely my identity, I'll be separated from half the human race; I'll identify myself in counter-distinction to women. The us and them distortion which follows from this exclusive biological identity will prevent me from finding happiness in the real world of persons.

If I identify my self on the bio-psychological level as heterosexual or homosexual, I will also be frustrated and disappointed. The gratification of my bio-psychological drives alone in any lifestyle cannot fulfill me personally, no matter how actively I pursue their gratification.

Only in meeting my personal need for intimacy can I bring a bit of happiness and fulfillment to my life in the area of sexuality. Only by identifying my *self* at the personal level and by using insight and freedom can I find meaning as a human being related to all other human beings. Only by the informed use of my insight and the non-manipulative use of my freedom in choosing behaviors which will provide intimacy in my life can I find personal meaning in my experience of being sexual.

A celibate commitment is possible for those whose sexual orientation is same-sex as well as for those who are other-sex oriented. A celibate commitment excludes for homosexually and heterosexually oriented people alike any attempt to make their *sexual* orientation their *life* orientation. A celibate commitment means I have decided to relate to no one through genital involvement and romantic pursuits. They are simply incompatible with a celibate life.

The labels and judgments we apply to our own and to other people's sexuality are among the most uncaring things we do to ourselves and to one another. Nowhere is this thoughtlessness more evident than when people who are dominantly other-sex oriented discuss the fitness for religious life and ordained ministry of someone who is thought to be same-sex oriented. The discussions are serious and the people are well-intentioned and sincere; the labels and judgments they use frustrate even their most dedicated efforts at understanding.

In discussing the fitness of a candidate for celibate life, I have adopted the practice of interchanging the labels "homosexual" and "heterosexual" in the questions which are raised. This has frequently led me to an examination of the issues involved beneath the labels, and helped me discover my own prejudices.

Some people object to such a practice in areas other than in discussions of the fitness of a candidate for the celibate life: "It isn't fair to impose on those oriented to their own sex the standards for behavior and understanding which are developed by and applied to people who are other-sex oriented." The assumption or the assertion which is frequently put forward in support of that position is that God made some people same-sex oriented and some people other-sex oriented, and God could not have intended only the other-sex oriented to find sexual fulfillment in romantic pursuits and genital involvements.

I disagree entirely with the argument because it is based on the *a priori* judgment that God intended some people to be same-sex oriented and some to be other-sex oriented; it also presumes that sexual fulfillment is achieved through biological and bio-psychological connecting with other human beings. The debate will rage for decades, and until the actual data of the experience of human sexual encounters is examined more significantly free of the influence of the stories we tell ourselves about those encounters, I don't expect a resolution. Nor do I think I have anything to contribute directly to it.

I use the technique of interchanging the terms homosexual and heterosexual because I believe that a celibate life does not include genital and romantic pursuits, and I do not presume either same-sex or other-sex oriented people are more prone than the other to romantic and genital behavior.

I am finding it increasingly difficult to give my opinion on the matter of the fitness of a candidate for a celibate life whose orientation is predominantly same-sex, precisely because my opinion on the matter can hardly ever be given by simply answering the questions which are posed. The questions range from "How many homosexuals can a community accept without becoming identified as a community of homosexuals?" to "How long prior to entry into novitiate must a homosexual candidate have refrained from homosexual activity?"

I have always taken the questions to be seriously asked by people who genuinely want to be just and understanding. My opinion usually cannot be expressed by a direct answer because it either says too little or implies too much. Even to accept the label homosexual as a substantive adjective already says more than I am willing to say. To say "three years" in answer to the "how long prior. . ." question doesn't say enough.

If I ask, for instance, how many heterosexuals can a community accept without becoming identified as a "heterosexual community," the underlying assumptions become a bit more clear.

The assumption about most communities is that their members are heterosexual, and yet it is unlikely that the community will be thought of as a "heterosexual community." That assumption does not come readily to conscious awareness when one speaks of a religious community. If it does come readily to awareness concerning a particular religious community, it would seem to do so for reasons other than the dominant sexual orientation of its members. Perhaps the members—or a significant number of its members—are making a point of their sexual orientation by their behavior or by their public expression of opinion. Perhaps their sexual orientation is orienting their life; perhaps the personal/spiritual commitment to a celibate lifestyle is no longer directing their behavior. I suspect that even one member of a religious community whose behavior—dress, activity, speech, manners, habits, haunts—was heterosexually oriented would be one too many. I suspect that even one religious who expressed opinions publicly about the right of the community members to have their need for heterosexual expression fulfilled in ways not accepted by the cultural mores would be unwelcome. If I am doing or advocating anything in terms of heterosexual behavior beyond that which the populace accepts as compatible with a celibate commitment, I will be suspect. And people probably won't want too many of me around! In fact, they'd probably wish I would go away!

The issue is not my heterosexual orientation; it's my *behavior* and my *public expression of opinion* about heterosexual behavior which is at issue. To be consistent, this must also be the issue regarding homosexual orientation.

Membership in the community is not the point; the point is a question of the likelihood that homosexually oriented people will be pressured by the politicized nature of the label into behaviors and public expression of opinion which are incompatible with a celibate religious commitment. Then the question might arise: "Is it serving the individual well to identify himself or herself by a label which derives from a bio-psychological reality; are we serving the person well by our trying to determine his or her fitness on the basis of the labels we are using in our discussion?" Whatever we think about accepting heterosexually oriented people into a community needs to be what we think about accepting homosexually oriented people. If a community is unwilling to use sexual labels for its members, then a candidate who insists on using sexual labels is probably not going to find happiness within the religious community. I think we make a mistake if we allow ourselves to be politically maneuvered away from a consistent viewpoint and to accept a different standard for the sexual minority.

"How long prior to making a celibate commitment should a person have abstained from homosexual activity?" Again, I do not advocate a separate standard for those who are homosexually oriented. For both heterosexually and homosexually oriented people I doubt that sexual abstinence is the issue. I believe the issue is more helpfully looked at in terms of sexual integration. A celibate lifestyle is a possibility for one who without great difficulty and without repression and denial has refrained from sexual activity for a minimum of three years—though I admit that is arbitrary. A person who has not engaged in extra-marital genital sexual behavior is the best candidate, not because of his or her sexual abstinence, but because that person is the one who has a chance of arriving at a consciously articulated appreciation of the meaning of human sexuality, and therefore is the best candidate for marriage or celibacy. If a person is not married and has engaged in sexual activity, he or she has already used another and/or has been used by another. Anyone who has done so in the recent past is not a likely candidate for religious life. So. . .a minimum of three years of not using people or being used by them gives some promise of living a celibate life, and living it as something more than sexual abstinence.

Pre-novitiate and seminary-type programs can be helpful to individuals in order to un-learn what may have been accepted as normative, provided that sexuality is dealt with directly and well. Using sexual labels and *a priori* judgments will probably not be helpful in such programs either.

Chapter 9
Intimacy Within Community

As the 25th anniversary of my first profession of vows fades quickly into history, I am very much aware that, like many before me, I could decide to leave religious life and the active ordained ministry. My exit story wouldn't be much different from those of close friends and people I admire and who have departed religious life.

As I've listened to people tell me their often tearful story of disenchantment with, or their decision to abandon further pursuit of a celibate life-commitment in the seminary or in initial religious formation, I've noticed two elements the narrations have in common. First, the stories they tell themselves tend to be generalized impressions gleaned from their experiences; and secondly, they most often select only the data of their experience which substantiates the story they are telling. I have no doubt that I would do the same were I in the process of leaving religious life. I have no doubt that I do the same now as I try to live religious life!

This phenomenon gives vivid testimony to the power the story has for leading us where we want to go. And that's largely the point of this and the following chapters: where we want to go most often determines how we interpret the data of our lives in the stories we tell ourselves and others!

The stories I've heard about why people leave usually center around their communities or the fraternity of diocesan priests with which they have exercised ministry. Frequently I have not concurred with the stories I have heard.

I don't mean these three chapters to be an exhortation or an instruction on how to stay committed to a celibate life. I don't present them to argue with those who have told themselves and me different stories about their ability to have their need for intimacy met within the celibate life-style. But I recognize that the stories are very influential ways in which we convince ourselves of the legitimacy or even the necessity of doing what we want to do. I know, because I tell myself some stories about the possibilities of meeting my need for intimacy within the celibate lifestyle, in my relationships with the members of my community, with people beyond my community and with God. I do so because I want to remain in religious life and the ordained ministry.

During my years of initial formation, I often heard a quote from Pope Pius XII. He said that a good community life is the greatest safeguard for the vow of chastity.

I took his words seriously, but understood them in a very exclusionary way. I thought he meant I should stay within the fold in forming my relationships. I should pray with my brothers, share meals with them and recreate in their company. His words implied that my interaction with people outside my community was to minister to them only. Social involvement with them would lead to emotional involvement, and that could lead to my violating my vow of chastity.

A quarter of a century later I still take Pius XII's words as seriously as I did when I was a novice, but I understand them a little differently.

Now I am one of the older members of my province and I feel much more responsible for the shape of my community life than I did when I was a novice. I take the Pope's words as an admonition to try to give that shape to our community life so my own and my brothers' need for intimacy can be met.

I don't suspect that even the best religious community or the most ideal diocesan fraternity of priests was ever meant to meet all the emotional and personal needs of its members. A priest or religious who expects or demands that his or her companions become "need-fulfillers" will become an intolerable burden to the rest. Yet we all come to religious life with a need for intimacy, and many of us have left because our need for intimacy has not been met. And most of us are inclined to attribute our leaving to anybody's failure but our own, even when we leave saying, "I guess I just wasn't cut out for that kind of life."

Part of the commitment to a celibate life is the decision to behave in ways which will allow my need for intimacy to be met. If I don't, I will be in jeopardy of abandoning the commitment.

I learned most of what I know about relationships within religious community from the novices with whom I lived and the people who chose to share with me their struggles as they approached leaving. They touched off my reflections on the dynamics of intimacy within the community.

During my first couple of years on the novitiate team I suffered through with the novices everything they suffered as they tried to become a community. It was as new to me as it was to them, and I was as confused and uncertain as they were. After a few years, however, I began to notice patterns or phases through which each class seemed to pass.

Our novitiate program got underway in mid-August with the "honeymoon" stage. From the time of their arrival through the first week of September everything was rosy. Games were brought out of the cupboards and the level of competition was always compatible with the cordiality which everybody needed to maintain. From my second floor window I could watch groups of novices walking together outside after supper and it looked like a picture of monastic bliss. Any task always attracted more volunteers than it could reasonably absorb.

From approximately the second week of September through mid-October the groups generally broke into pairs as the novices seemed to single out classmates for private conversations. It was the "I want to get to know you" stage. The games were put back into the cupboard for the following year's class to discover, as novices went about discovering who these classmates were.

This phase would inevitably be followed by the "practical joke" stage. I began to regard it as an extension of the "I want to get to know you" phase, but with a twist. Two or more of the novices would think up some prank to play on a classmate to see how he'd react. Usually around the end of October somebody's feelings got pretty severely hurt, and by my third or fourth year on the novitiate staff I tried to be away from the house for Halloween!

During November I tried to teach something about community living skills and the whole staff got very serious about directing the novices in their personal reflection and prayer. Prior to November it would have been useless to do so; but after the polite honeymoon stage and the private conversations of the "I want to get to know you" stage, and the failure of the practical jokes to bring about the contact with one another they all desired, the novices were usually ready for some guidance in reflecting on the dynamics which had taken place within and among us since mid-August.

As I have experienced it, it is not possible for one person to "get to know" another if the other won't allow it. But I can allow others to know me. My problem is that sometimes my own self-awareness may not be very great, so I am limited in my self-disclosure.

Time off by myself may allow me to reflect on my activity and to begin to see that my behavior is frequently automatic response to the feelings I have about an event I've experienced. Many people, if asked why they behaved the way they did, say something like, "Well, when you didn't invite me to go shopping with you, you made me angry, so I couldn't talk to you at the table."

It was only after I had long since left the novitiate team that I was introduced to a way of understanding the dynamics at work within me as I experience different events generating a variety of feelings which prompt my behavior.

As automatic as it may seem, an event does not produce a feeling in me. *You* don't "make me feel" anything. The same event can generate in me different feelings depending on the attitudes and assumptions I have about life. Frequently I don't know these attitudes so I can be mystified by the feelings which are generated by the events I experience.

For instance, I feel absolutely helpless and very angry when I need to take my car to a dealer for repair. As I drive into the service department I feel like a sheep being led to slaughter. I immediately begin to act gruff—not characteristic of me—and pretend to know a lot more than I really do about what needs to be done to my car. I have an assumption—not entirely unfounded—that I'm going to be ripped off by the car dealer. I assume all dealers are my adversaries. My affective level has been educated by past experience and only further experiences will change my assumption about dealers.

But dealers don't really "make me feel" helpless, threatened and angry. I feel that way because of my attitude toward them. But I don't know that unless I take some time to reflect on my feelings and attitudes.

Feeling threatened, helpless and angry, I behave gruffly and impolitely toward the service manager, no matter how friendly he or she might try to be. It seems like an automatic response, but it isn't. It's very spontaneous and by now habitual, but it is not automatic. Only if I reflect on my behavior and look to see what other options are open to me will I be in a position to change this behavior.

If I could slow down the internal processes, I could see that even when I feel angry and threatened, acting gruff and pretending to know more than I do is "bargain basement" behavior. I'm going to invest a good deal of energy in being sort of nasty and in pretending, and I'm not going to get anything worthwhile in return for that investment of energy. By reflecting on my behavior I can see that it is a poor investment and that there are other options. I could tell the service representative that I'm fearful of bringing my car in. I could ask questions about what needs to be done instead of pretending I know what the matter is. I could ask for help instead of being an adversary.

So what does all this have to do with creating strategies to meet my needs for intimacy within my religious community or within the fraternity of priests with whom I serve the diocese? Just this: The same spontaneous reactions go on in me when I'm faced with any event in community life. If I am going to understand myself, I need to be aware of the feelings events generate in me, and through reflection come to know the attitudes I espouse, often unconsciously. If I am unaware of most of what goes on in me and really believe that others "make me feel" as I do: if I believe I have no control of my behavior because of how someone else "made me feel," I am attempting to credit or blame other members of my community with the success or failure of my religious life. Someday I may tell my exit story as a tale of other people's failure.

My relationships within my community or with the bishop and other priests of the diocese depend on them as well as myself. I have no control over what they do, but if I increase my level of self-awareness I am better prepared to let them know me. And that self-disclosure can be the initiation of an intimate relationship within community.

I've sometimes thought of members of a religious community or of the priests of a diocese as a batch of donuts floating on the surface of the vat of oil. The different thicknesses of the donuts represent different levels of self-awareness and self-disclosure. There is a center of each one of us which remains unknown to us. But some of us are "fatter" with self-awareness and self-disclosure than others.

I've imagined that occasionally there is one so slender in

self-awareness and self-disclosure as to be almost invisible among the others. Invisible as that one is, it can exist in the middle of a ring of donuts and keep the others apart.

The person who does not disclose himself or herself becomes the mystery in our midst, and we don't live comfortably with a mystery in our midst. We want to know that person. For lack of self-disclosure we begin to psyche him or her out. We begin to use our own imaginations to try to fill in the gaps, to make the person the object of our scrutiny and speculation. "What makes that person tick? What goes on inside?" the others begin to ask themselves first and then one another. And soon everyone is talking *about* the person instead of *to* the person.

The mystery person affects the way all of us come together—or don't come together. The person may have a support system outside the community. But there are limits to how minimal that self-disclosure in community can be without turning it into a purely functional arrangement.

Religious who remain a mystery do a disservice to their community. Those who try to psyche out the mystery persons also make a mistake, because they make them an object of their scrutiny and thereby increase the likelihood of their choosing to alienate themselves permanently.

When I try to "get to know you," I may invite you to alienate yourself, because you become for me an object of my curiosity and scrutiny. I think of the "I want to get to know you" syndrome as the dynamics of alienation. When I let you know me, however, I may invite you to a similar self-awareness and self-disclosure because the experience or behavior which I disclose to you can put you in touch with your own experience or behavior. Our mutual self-disclosure can allow intimacy to arise among us.

Married and celibate life are significantly different. But in the matter of these dynamics I have witnessed similarities between the way spouses have related to each other and the ways priests in rectories have related to each other and the ways religious relate in communities. And I have come to think of them as the mistake which is available to everybody.

Two priests produced the same entangled relationship between themselves that we often encounter between a husband and wife. Within the same week both priests stopped into my office to tell me about their difficulties which were spilling over into their ministry within the parish. Each cried as he spoke about the likelihood of transferring to a different parish.

In the course of their separate narrations each spoke about hurtful behavior of the other. Father Leon, let me call him, told about Father Daniel's criticizing him in front of some parishioners one Sunday morning between Masses. Father Daniel told me of Father Leon's insistence on the candles being left lit between the Masses and sort of generally telling him how to do most things. Each one was very much aware of the other's behavior.

Despite each one's pain neither condemned the other. "I can understand where he's coming from," Father Leon said. "He's young and enthusiastic and needs to prove himself." And Father Daniel was equally understanding: "He's a good man but he's threatened by my popularity in the parish." Each one has psyched the other out and "understood" what motivated the other.

Neither priest gave evidence of being in touch with his own behavior; neither reported any cognizance of his own feelings or attitudes; and neither seemed aware of any changes he could make to improve the situation. The bishop eventually transferred one of them and they parted company telling the story of the other's failure. The dynamics of alienation had worked their way out to their conclusion in the lives of two dedicated ministers.

Father Leon, in speaking about the whole matter some months later, revealed another dynamic he used and which almost guarantees he'll have similar experiences in the future. I call it the dynamics of isolation.

He spoke about some of *his own* behaviors and he concluded by saying, "That's just the way I am." His tone reinforced his words; they sounded like, "I don't intend to change the way I behave."

In counselling a man about difficulties in his family life, Jerry heard him repeat more times than he wanted to endure, "That's just the way I am." Each time the man came for his weekly appointment, Jerry helped him see that his behavior was "bargain basement," and was contributing to the deterioration of his family life. It became increasingly clear to the man that what he needed to do and wanted to do would cost him more effort than he was accustomed to putting forward, but it could possibly improve his home situation. "Then why do you continue to act the way you do?" Jerry asked. "Because that's just the way I am," the man said without hesitation.

Jerry got out of his chair and said, "C'mon. Follow me."

"Where are we going?" the man asked.

"You'll see," Jerry said. He walked out the front door of the friary and led the man to the cemetery across the street.

"I don't like cemeteries," the man said. "They give me the willies."

"Well, you might just as well get used to the cemetery," Jerry said, "That's where you're living most of your life. Everybody here could say 'That's just the way I am,' and it would be accurate. They can't change because they're dead. If you want to continue counselling with me, you leave instructions in your will that they should engrave on your tombstone: THAT'S JUST THE WAY I AM, because it will be true of you when you're dead; but don't ever say that to yourself or to me again because you are choosing to live in a cemetery. Counselling dead people is a waste of my time."

In rectories and religious communities lots of people choose to tell themselves the story of their inability to change their behavior by saying, "Well, that's just the way I am."

The statement frequently represents a refusal to be affected by the self-disclosure of those with whom they live.

"I'm uncomfortable with the amount you drink." "Well, that's just the way I am."

"I'm nervous about the way you drive." "Well, that's just the way I am."

"I feel put down when you criticize me in public." "Well, that's just the way I am."

"I get lonely when we just sit here and watch TV instead of talking to each other." "Well, after being on the job all day, that's all I can do."

"I wish we could pray together once in a while." "I don't get anything out of praying in common."

The words vary, but the message is the same.

The dynamics of alienation by which I do not disclose myself and the dynamics of isolation by which I refuse to be affected by what others disclose to me, can go on amid lots of chatter and banter and very successful functional living within the religious community or the rectory. The activities I used to observe among novices at the beginning of the novitiate year—the politeness, the joking, the psyching out, the conversations about instead of with another—can go on for years before it catches up with people. But after sufficient time, people often begin to realize that something is missing from their lives.

Beneath their success and popularity, they discover a hunger for intimacy in their lives. The better a person has been at being unrevealing and unreceptive of another's disclosure and the longer that has gone on along with politeness, banter and chatter, the ruder the awakening. The most "popular" and "successful" seem at times to be gone the quickest, as they pursue the beginnings of intimacy in a budding romantic relationship. The exit story, no matter how tearfully told, is one of the community's failure to meet a member's need for intimacy, and the ability of the new relationship to provide what has been missing.

I don't remember hearing much recrimination in the stories people have told me as they departed religious life or the active ordained ministry; there's only sadness and regret. The sadness has been compounded for those who experienced warmth and feeling from those they told about their decision to leave. "I never knew they cared for me that much," one religious sobbed as she told of the tearful parting she experienced with the sisters in her community. "If there had been more of that throughout the last 15 years, I might not have decided to leave. Now it's too late."

The pain I felt with her didn't change the fact that I told myself a different story about why she decided to leave. I'm sure it was true that the other members of her community hadn't revealed their care and affection as clearly as they did when she disclosed her pain in leaving and her recognition of a need to be cared for. But the other sisters revealed what was in them in response to her self-disclosure. Perhaps she would not have decided to leave if she had recognized her need for intimacy and disclosed some of the significant data of her life, her feelings and her need. Perhaps, just perhaps, they would have responded to her as they did when she was leaving them. She'll never know.

Occasionally I've heard it said that a certain religious is very institutionalized. The statement has usually been made as a commentary on the individual's apparent inability to relate personally to the rest of the community. It may also be a description of the person's dependence on structures, schedules and role expectations. Any change in the institutionalized structures seems to cause a rather severe reaction. I tend to attribute the anger and withdrawal in an "institutionalized" religious to the loss of connectedness caused by a change in the structures.

Each of us needs to feel safe and related if we are to have a sense of connectedness with others. In an "institutionalized" model of connectedness, our sense of safety is achieved because we feel protected or taken care of; our sense of being related comes largely from filling roles which relate to the roles filled by others. Provincial, local superior, novice, pastor, teacher, formation team member, newly professed, newly ordained, bishop, chancellor—these and many other roles are related to one another and we relate to one another because we fill those roles.

In the "personalized" model of connectedness, our sense of safety comes from feeling appreciated or cared for; our sense of being related comes from the intimacy we experience with others.

Lack of feeling safe and related is a major contributing factor in almost everyone's decision to leave religious life. Some in religious life get their sense of safety and relatedness from a predominantly institutionalized model, others from a predominantly personalized model. Those whose sense of safety and relatedness comes primarily from an institutionalized model can hardly understand why someone leaves religious life. Leaving religious life or the active ordained ministry because he or she doesn't feel appreciated or intimate is almost unfathomable to the "institutionalized" priest or religious. And the fidelity to commitment shown by those who get their sense of safety and relatedness from the role they fill and from being protected is a mystery to those who hunger for intimacy and appreciation.

When institutionalized religious get a taste of the personalized sense of safety and relatedness from someone outside the community they can leave very suddenly because the taste of this new reality seems so far superior to their experience up to now. They easily consider religious life or the ordained ministry the reason why they have never experienced intimacy before. But it is the way they have lived religious life or engaged in ordained ministry which has deprived them of the experience of being safe and related in personal ways.

In religious life and in the fraternity of priests within a

diocese, I believe we are in a transition from a predomi-nantly institutionalized model of connectedness to a more personalized model. The sense of connectedness which we get from a predominantly institutionalized model has faded; many of us now feel insufficiently taken care of and pro-tected because we are less sure of the significance of the roles we fill, and so we no longer feel as much a part of the prov-ince or the diocese. Many of us have not yet made the transi-tion to a more personalized model which comes from being appreciated and from allowing intimacy to arise among us.

To be sure, some of us do not want to make the transi-tion; we are inclined to call ourselves and our brothers and sisters back to what used to be. Many of us want to make the transition, but we are not yet comfortable with the required skills.

I don't suspect that religious life or the diocesan priest-hood can exist as a totally institutionalized entity; it never has. Nor do I look forward to the day when our whole sense of connectedness with one another is exclusively personal-ized; that would take too much energy to sustain. We need a balance, but today the balance needs to be tipped in favor of a more personal approach to our connectedness.

All intimacy includes the sense that I know I am known because I have made myself known and I am accepted as I have revealed myself. There is a connectedness brought about because of being known and accepted.

Intimacy takes time to grow. It can begin unexpectedly and needs only to be nourished by the dynamics of self-awareness and self-disclosure in the hearing of another. Inti-mate relationships develop a history, and each intimate rela-tionship has its own history of connectedness.

Ideally, our family provides a sense of connectedness whose history is the longest. I was myself and I revealed my-self to my parents and family long before I was free to choose to do so. There was and remains an institutional connectedness that comes from belonging to my family. With minimal nourishment that connectedness endures and can sustain neglect better than relationships established later in life. It can be nourished by simply "going home," provided "home" is more than a building.

Even after a person has established a home of one's own, the sense of connectedness to parents, brothers, sisters, grandparents, aunts and uncles and cousins can continue to be a primary experience of connectedness. The death of members of the previous generations need not destroy the connectedness if the intimacy among siblings and family is nourished.

The withdrawal of celibate religious and priests from their parental home is much the same as that of their married siblings. So is their connectedness to that home as long as it lasts. But their establishment of a home of their own differs. Religious life and diocesan priesthood are not families and cannot be in the same sense as married people. But the kind of primary relationships which are associated with family need to be established with the religious community or the diocesan priesthood. *Intimacy with a history* is required.

The kind of connectedness which is appropriate and necessary is akin to that which we experienced in our childhood home and which we would experience with our spouses and children if we had married. The sense of being safe and related through a balance of institutional and personal bonds needs to be established. Without it, something which most people crave is lacking. In this kind of setting—whether connected to a particular place or not—is where we can take it for granted that we belong. If this primary connectedness is neglected or absent from the life of priests or religious, they will continually look for it in the setting of their ministry, an inappropriate setting in which to look. Ministry can be the setting to develop intimate relationships with many people, even intimate relationships which last a lifetime and develop their own history of connectedness. But it is not and cannot be the setting for the connectedness which is simply *taken for granted* because one belongs in that primary way which is typical of family ties.

Home for priests and religious most often cannot be related to a particular place; it is connected rather to the other members of their primary community, those with whom they feel "at home" wherever they are. It is helpful for priests and religious to be able to leave the scene of their ministry and "go home" even if it is to gather at a rented cottage with other priests and religious for a vacation, a day off, or a special celebration.

Joint ventures in ministry between members of different religious communities, or between diocesan priests and religious, or among lay people, religious and diocesan priests simply do not serve as home for anyone in the sense of primary relatedness, because the dissolution of the institutional bonds which connect the ministers can be brought about by many circumstances. The termination of a contract, a transfer, a decision to opt out of the arrangement will send each person home to some place where the connectedness of belonging is not dependent on contracts, working arrangements or free decision on the part of all to remain connected. Home is where the connectedness of belonging can sustain my incapacitation, my eccentricities, even my obstinate refusal to cooperate.

I have witnessed collaborative ventures in ministry among people from different groups. Those which have seemed most successful are those in which none of the ministers has tried to make the ministry setting the place of his or her primary connectedness. Those which have been least successful are those which included some ministers who sought their primary sense of belonging from the group. The simple fact that someone had no place "to go home to" placed emotional burdens on the rest and expectations which could not be met.

Religious community or the diocesan fraternity of priests *can be* settings in which a sense of being safe and related achieves the balance of institutional and personal elements that home implies. There all can belong.

The last quarter century has witnessed a decline in the ability of institutionalized connectedness to hold priests and religious together. Our society, our church, and most religious communities are inviting us to a more predominantly "personalized" connectedness with one another. That requires us to be willing to deal with the issues of intimacy and to learn behaviors which will allow it to arise among us. Without that we will no longer have much of anything binding us together.

If I need to feel appreciated in order to feel safe in the personalized model, then others must communicate that appreciation to me.

Appreciation for one another exists within religious communities and among diocesan priests. However, it is often not communicated, or is communicated obliquely, or submerged under the competition which also exists. The institutionalized model has such a hold on us—or we hold on so firmly to it—that we seldom verbally and emotionally offer one another the appreciation we need to feel safe. We rely on discharging our duties in the roles we fill, much like Tevye in "Fiddler on the Roof" who listed all he did as a husband and a provider when his wife asked "Do you love me?"

Given the occasion to speak to or about the one whom we appreciate, we may jest, ridicule, belittle or discount that person verbally, relying on the institutionalization we experience to correct the impression our words must inevitably give. "I was just kidding," is the self-absolution and reparation we offer.

Our verbal abuse can, after a while, erode the value of our action in behalf of one another. It can destroy the sense of safety we seek to establish with our actions.

When we do verbalize our gratitude and appreciation, we frequently select a mode of speaking which reflects our bias for an institutionalized manner of relating. "That was a great dinner," usually is an attempt to express gratitude for the meal and appreciation for the one who prepared it. But verbally it is a judgment about the quality of the meal. The recipient can usually quite readily translate the words of judgment about the meal into sentiments of gratitude and appreciation unless he or she is already feeling alienated from the speaker.

Judgments about the quality of another's performance or about another's personal characteristics may be favorable, and they may stem from sentiments of gratitude and appreciation. They are needed from time to time to bolster confidence. They do not, however, tell the other anything directly about the sentiments of the speaker. "Thank you!" and "I appreciate what you've done for me!" would do so.

Direct expressions of gratitude and appreciation help a person feel cared for and therefore safe. And if I receive such a direct expression I need to be careful not to deflect it into a statement about my performance or abilities. Deflecting "thank you for dinner" into "that was a great meal," is to cling to the institutionalized model of obtaining the sense of safety I need. We also need appreciation if we are going to feel safe in a personal way with those to whom we are connected in religious life or ordained ministry.

The words we use in our dealing with one another reveal something about which model of connectedness is dominant for us. Those who are primarily institutionalized tend to say rather frequently, "*I* have a right to. . ." and therefore "*You* should. . . ." Those who are more personalized in their attitudes and activities tend to say more often, "*I'm* grateful for. . ." and "Thank *you*."

Dealing with intimacy in our lives as priests and religious will not put an end to people leaving religious life or the active ordained ministry. Nor will it mean that communities of religious and fraternities of priests will cease to experience tension.

But the stories we tell ourselves are important instruments in helping us go where we want to go. I tell myself that it is possible to behave in ways which will allow intimacy to arise within religious communities and among diocesan priests because I want to pursue those possibilities instead of looking elsewhere to have my need for intimacy met. I have intimate relationships beyond those I have with my brothers in the Order; I would not feel comfortable were I to have intimate relationships with others instead of with those to whom I find myself committed by bonds of religious profession. That might leave me with only institutionalized bonds of connectedness with them; those alone don't seem to hold us together in helpful and healthy ways.

Chapter 10
Intimacy Beyond My Community

I used to be afraid of close personal relationships with people beyond the borders of my community. My fear was reinforced by those who spoke of the danger of such relationships especially if they were with a person of the other sex. That could lead only to trouble for the person with a celibate commitment. The celibate heart was given to God, the reasoning went; allowing someone else even the chance to gain access to a piece of that limited resource was flirting with infidelity. "God is a jealous lover," more than one retreat master admonished.

In my first years of ordained ministry, I was usually very cordial to the people with whom and to whom I ministered. However, I held firmly on to the notion that some sort of separation ought to be maintained between me and those whom I greeted so cordially after Mass on Sunday.

I still remember vividly the Sunday evening I first walked unannounced into the home of a man who has since become a dear friend. After Sunday Mass Jim had often said to "stop in sometime." It was clear in my own mind as I walked up the porch steps that I was doing so not as Father Keith, the cordial young priest. It was as Keith Clark, a man feeling lonely that evening. I was crossing a self-imposed barrier into dangerous territory.

I remember nothing of the details of the evening's visit. I presume it resembled my frequent visits over the next seven years. There was never any fuss over my arrival. "How 'bout a drink, Clark?"—to which I was always free to respond, "No thanks, Jim."—eventually became a standard part of the introductory rite, but I'm sure that first visit must have begun a little more formally.

Neither do I have any recollections of my return home that evening, but because it was the way I did things, I presume I told the other members of the novitiate staff of my visit and its significance. I did not present my activity for their approval or disapproval, and they offered neither. It was important to me, though, that they knew what I was doing.

Two years after I was assigned to the novitiate, I was appointed the head of the team. That placed on me responsibilities which I felt as an increased burden, but I enjoyed it most of the time. There were days and nights, however, when all I wanted to do was to escape everything about the novitiate. I frequently escaped to the Parkers. I never passed up an invitation to a party celebrating Jim's or Eloise's or one of their seven children's birthdays. Even without anything so specific occasioning my visit, I continued to visit regularly until it became part of my weekly ritual. The social highlight of my week was having tea with Eloise one afternoon each week.

I knew from the beginning that it was for me that I visited the Parkers. I also sensed that I could not make them a substitute for my community connectedness; nor could I depend on their company as the sole source of my social life beyond my community. Having crossed the self-imposed barrier, and having experienced none of the undesirable consequences I had anticipated, I broadened the range of my social involvement beyond my community. Each Sunday evening I'd go for a walk through town and frequently I'd stop in some home for a visit. The benefit of doing so became obvious, although I could articulate nothing of what that benefit was.

I was certain enough that my contacts and growing friendships were good for me. On many occasions when I was quite sure that my opinion on some matter would not carry very much weight with one of the novices, I'd suggest that he go and talk with Jim and Eloise, or Tom and Ann, or Don and Mary, or with whatever family in town he had become friends with. The other members of the novitiate team developed their own friends and the social connectedness between the friars and the neighbors grew. This seemed to enhance the way we worshipped together on Sundays.

When I first began presiding at Eucharist each Sunday, I studied and reflected on the scriptures for the day so in my homily I could tell the congregation what the scriptures could mean to their lives. As the years passed I realized the scriptures had meaning *for me* because of what I knew of the lives of those who gathered for Eucharist. At the beginning I tried to tell the folks how the Good News could find a place in their lives; by the time I left that place, the Good News I announced in my homily was what I could see of God already at work in their lives and mine.

Not long before I was transferred I was at a party in the Parker home. As always it centered on the dining room table, and it was very lively with the comings and goings of friends of various members of the family. In the middle of the partying and laughter, one of Jim's and Eloise's children gave me a big hug and said, "We did a good job on you."

"What do you mean?" I asked with some misgiving.

"Oh, when you came to town, you were so uptight and self-conscious. Now you know how to just be yourself."

My initial inclination was to argue the point: I had *not* been uptight and self-conscious when I arrived; I had been cordial, gracious and very friendly! But as I scanned my memory—from my first visit, my weekly tea with Eloise, brandy manhattans with Jim, the tears and anger, the tensions and the frustrations they had let me in on, and those I had shared with them—I said, "Yeah, I guess you did."

Having entered a supposedly forbidden territory, I found it not to be an area fraught with danger, but, like the rest of my life, a hospitable and supportive arena with the same pitfalls as my life within my community.

As I allowed people to know me and as they let me know them, a certain role-related distance between us began to disappear. The gap which we had presumed to be separating us was not horizontal, but vertical. Because I was a priest and religious, we all supposed I breathed the thinner air of an elevated position. I believed the elevation, no matter how I might minimize it, was part of the safeguard of my celibate commitment. At first I could not articulate the benefit I was sure I was getting from my contact with people beyond my community. Now I think that a mutual respect was growing among us.

"Respect" mean literally "to look again," to re-examine the assumptions and prejudices we have about ourselves and others. I was growing in my ability to look again at myself and at the people with whom I was connecting in bonds of personal intimacy. I knew already that people beyond my community appreciated a priest or religious whose "feet were on the ground." I don't think that prevented them or me from assuming that the ground upon which my feet were planted was elevated somewhat above the ground upon which they stood. As we each allowed the other to know who we were we saw that we stood on the common plain of human existence.

Because of the respect I developed for those with whom I share the common experience of being human and because we allowed one another to come to know one another in our chosen lives, I felt strengthened and supported in my celibate commitment.

The distance supposedly existing between a celibate person and those called to other lifestyles is probably a threat to a celibate life, not a safeguard. When celibate men and women and others beyond their communities reinforce the notion of some elevated distance between them, then celibates can think they are made of some "stuff" different from their brothers and sisters. They can begin to rely on this stuff—whatever it is—to help support their celibate commitment, instead of carefully selecting behaviors which make up the lifestyle they are pursuing. By carefully discerning behaviors which are compatible with and nourishing of our lifestyle we safeguard our commitment to marriage, the single life or the celibate life.

"Familiarity breeds contempt" can keep priests and religious scrambling for that imaginary elevated ground. Familiarity breeds contempt only for those who, in their own lack of self-awareness and self-acceptance, suspect that they are worthy of it and therefore try to hide themselves behind some facade of superiority, or for those who live their lives among the care-less. The role-related expectations of priests and religious invite them to try to be superhuman and to maintain a distance from other people. This used to guarantee that they would be protected from contamination, even by those presumed to be the contaminants. But priests and religious can starve to death personally in that rarefied institutionalized atmosphere. Sharing the familiar plains of human existence can provide the setting in which celibate men and women can be cared for by those for whom they care.

I do not suppose that most people among whom I live are uncaring of me and my lifestyle. Their care has protected me from that elevated and self-sufficient stance, which is false, and from which I would fall if I relied on some imaginary "stuff" to keep me faithful. I could become care-less of myself and of my celibate commitment by choosing behaviors which were not nurturing of my commitment.

In visiting homes of friends beyond my community I learned that the plains of humanity are friendly and I can trust their care of me. I can also entrust myself and my celibate call to the care of my brothers and sisters by behaving toward them in ways which allow intimacy to arise among us.

In order to experience that fusing and counterpointing of personalities of which intimacy is made up, I have to come together with others in ways which insure that all of us remain intact. If I present myself as one who is care-full—not only in the sense of cautious—of the celibate life, I will invite a similar care from others. If I show myself to be care-less of the gift of my vocation, I can expect that they will receive me that way and will behave toward me in equally care-less ways. The pitfalls in the land beyond my community are there because I bring them with me.

By now it is clear that I am convinced that it is our behaviors and our stories which are the important elements in pursuing a celibate commitment. I am further convinced that I will choose the behaviors and tell myself the stories I do in order to help me pursue the path I want to pursue. Those who are victims of disillusionment and who have abandoned their celibate commitment are, in my experience, usually willing victims. Some were willing victims because in their religious communities or in the fraternity of priests they experienced almost nothing which met their need for intimacy. Some tried to behave in ways which would allow intimacy to arise and met only with behaviors which were intolerably impersonal because they relied on institutionalized approaches to the connectedness which held them together. As a result they were starving to death as persons. Others left a life they never really wanted but which they allowed themselves to be talked into by well-meaning and highly motivated people. The majority of us, though, who have left religious life or the ordained ministry did so because of the behaviors we chose and the stories we told ourselves about our need for intimacy.

Occasionally I have met people who do not have care for my commitment to a celibate life. Those people behaved toward me in ways which were romantic. If I find such a person attractive I am tempted to want to reciprocate. What has safeguarded and supported my celibate commitment is not withdrawal from further contact with people beyond my community; it has been safeguarded and supported when I could entrust myself and my life to the scrutiny of those who care for me—both in and beyond my community.

I have fallen in love seriously once in my religious life. My romantic and genital inclinations could have led me to leave my commitment. I suspect they would have, had I not told those to whom I was committed by bonds of religious profession what I was experiencing, and had I concentrated all my significant self-disclosure on the woman I was in love with. When I feel romantically inclined toward someone, my romantic feelings can almost seduce me to disclose what is most personal about myself. I am inclined to tell that person that I am "in love," and I am equally inclined to hide the fact from all others. Yet I think the worst thing I can do is to "go underground" with my relationship, because I remove myself from the possibility of care of those who support me in my celibate commitment. I can begin to tell myself those stories by which I deny that I am behaving in response to my urges and drives.

"I am meeting this person because she needs it."

"I am not telling anyone what we are doing, because they are too narrow-minded to see that this is the way people should behave toward each other."

"We're only doing what everybody should do if they weren't so uptight."

"Well, at least we're not. . . ."

These are the clues that I'm choosing romantic behaviors and telling myself stories which will not support my celibate commitment.

If I focus my attention exclusively on the person who has become the object of my fascination, I deprive myself of the support of others and begin to rely on that superhuman "stuff" of which I think I am made in order to remain faithful to my celibate commitment. Disaster is predictable.

I know of no priest or religious who consciously sought

to become romantically involved with another. And those who did, did so without any intention of abandoning their celibate commitment. The narrations I have listened to are filled with passive phrases such as: "We were swept along by our romance until eventually we found ourselves in bed with each other."

I think those statements are more true than I used to be willing to believe. Behaviors have consequences. Romantic activity suggests we would like to pursue the possibility of choosing each other as mates. That meaning may not be intended, but it cannot be escaped. The romantic relationship almost impels the people to genital involvement or demands that the relationship be broken off altogether. If the people who are romantically involved have had intercourse, a promise has been made to be there for each other in the future. At that point a celibate man or woman finds himself or herself in an entirely untenable position of having two contrary commitments. And it's often not until then that the relationship is brought "above ground" and the predicament is shared with a trusted friend.

I have anguished with several people who have found themselves with a public commitment to religious life or the priesthood and a private commitment to someone with whom they have had a romantic and genital relationship for some time. No, they never intended things to go as far as they have; no, they don't want to leave their religious or priestly commitment; no, they don't want to break off the relationship entirely; no, the lover is not demanding that they leave religious life or the priesthood; no, they don't think they can keep seeing the person without continuing to have sex; no, they don't know what to do. That's anguish!

I still feel the anguish in them and in myself. I spent four or five months in fairly regular conversation with a friend in that situation, and was very discouraged. When another person wanted to talk to me about a romantic and genital relationship "he found himself in" I was unwilling to suffer through "another one." When he came to talk I listened to the regretfully familiar opening lines about "I think I have to leave religious life because I'm involved with a woman," and the stories of how gradual and inevitable the evolution of the relationship seemed. I said something I thought I would regret later. "Stop! How do you want this to turn out?"

"Well, I'm not sure," was the thoughtful reply.

"Then don't talk to me about it yet, because in telling me the story you'll also be telling yourself for the first time out loud; and the way you tell the story will determine to a large extent how this will resolve. You have three options: continue to pursue two contrary commitments, end the romantic and genital relationship and pursue only your celibate life, or leave religious life to pursue only the other commitment. Until you know what you want to do, don't tell me or yourself any stories." I frightened myself with the vehemence and conviction with which I spoke.

He thought for quite a while, and I was sure I had blown it. I knew in my heart that I was protecting myself from more anguish. Eventually he said, "I want to stay in my community, I guess."

"Not good enough," I said, feeling like a real ogre. "When you know which exit you want to take out of this mess, I'll be glad to listen."

The hour was approaching midnight when he said that he wanted to remain in his religious community. I invited him to tell me precisely how the relationship had developed. In response to my own frustration at having listened to another brother tell me in generalities about the way his relationship had developed and why, I said, "Start at the beginning and just tell me the data. Tell me what I would l have seen and heard had I been along with you, right up to your decision to speak to me tonight. Tell me what you felt, what

you thought at the time, what you said and how you behaved. Tell me what you did together."

"I met her at a bar I went to after a movie. I was feeling lonely. I needed to be held by someone because the guys
I live with don't communicate with me. I. . . ."

"Stop, please! Those are stories you are telling yourself
about yourself and others. For now just go over the data. After we have a picture of what happened, we'll go back over
it all and lay over whatever story you want and together
we'll look to see if it fits the data."

I didn't want to get entangled in interpretations and
generalities again. As self-serving as my intention was, it
seemed also to serve my friend quite well. By two o'clock in
the morning he concluded that he had behaved foolishly in
light of the fact that he wanted to live a celibate life and
that he had been telling himself stories all along in order to
justify his behavior. Those stories he had told himself just
didn't fit the data and so he abandoned them.

The stories I have so often heard center around the way
the "other made me feel," the meaning a response to another
had, and what would all but inevitably follow from having
been made to feel that way. The conclusion to the stories has
frequently been that the individual would have been better
off never having gotten involved with people outside the
community. The exit stories are the same ones I'm sure I'd
tell myself were I intending to leave: "My community failed
to provide me with what I need, and someone beyond my
community has provided it." I doubt that I'd take any more
responsibility for my behavior than others have done as they
left religious life or the active ordained ministry.

Many myths surround relationships between men and
women and there are not many models for relationships
which do not include romantic involvement. The same
myths spill over onto those who are predominantly oriented
to their own sex; and they too lack models for non-romantic
relationships. The myths suggest that there is no real inti-

macy that is not romantic and genital. Even those relationships between men and women who are saints are considered "special" and "spiritual," and beyond the realm of what ordinary human beings can hope to attain. Those myths need to be dismantled.

A phone conversation late one night with Dennis brought some clarity to thoughts which had been only confused before. Dennis complained—as I have at times—that he grows tired of living in an open and sharing way and not experiencing any return in kind from others. He also said, "And I don't have a Jan in my life!"

It struck me then and makes sense to me now, that those who are unresponsive to another's attempt at disclosure are the losers. And those who share their lives benefit from the behavior, even without reciprocal self-disclosure. We cannot predict or control another's response. But if one in a hundred responds, a friend can be made.

I told Dennis that I hoped he realized too that there is no difference between my friendship with him or with Jerry or Ron or Paul and my relationship with Jan. The kind of relationship which exists between Jan and me is the same as the kind which exists between Dennis and me. Relationships are based on the kinds of behavior people choose, not on what goes on inside of them.

Relationships with those whom I do find initially attractive can be allowed to grow in the same way as those with people whom I found initially unattractive. I do not have to behave romantically toward those whom I find attractive any more than I have to behave rudely toward those whom I don't like initially. I can choose behaviors which are self-disclosing and accepting of the disclosure of another without doing so just to continue a biological or biopsychological stimulation. I may be romantically inclined and even genitally stimulated by another and still refrain from romantic and genital behaviors. For many celibate people, some relationships are romantic in their effect, but a celibate commitment excludes only behaving in ways which are romantic by design. It is only those who tell themselves the story that romantic feelings and genital inclinations must motivate their behavior who necessarily regard contact with attractive people beyond their community as a threat to their celibate commitment.

I am saddened by the choice of behaviors of some who ruin the chances for intimate relationships beyond their community. Remaining isolated and aloof is one way people ruin the possibilities of relationships. Giving off mixed messages about their seriousness about pursuing their celibate commitment is another way of squelching a budding intimate relationship; they behave romantically the moment they *feel* romantic, and therefore in the fusing of personalities which they seek, they surrender part of themselves. What could have developed into an intimate relationship becomes a problem because behaving romantically is incompatible with a life commitment. A third way people sabotage the chances for intimate relationships to grow is by demanding that others meet our needs for emotional stimulation and support. We become emotional leeches which people will cast off as soon as they recognize what we are doing to them.

Relationships frequently are not allowed the time they need to develop to the point of intimacy, because people begin to demand of each other—usually very subtly—that they meet their need for intimacy. People need to cultivate their ability to be grateful and appreciative of others until they reach the point where they recognize that they have come to need each other because of what they have already given by being themselves. If we concentrate on our own urges and drives and need for intimacy, and begin to subtly or overtly make demands on another, the relationship will never reach the intimacy which could have existed between us.

I have never been able to come up with specific do's and don'ts for what I consider appropriate behavior for celibate people in relationships. I suspect that if I could, they would resemble very closely the do's and don't which married people observe in their relationships with all but their spouses. Genital activity is incompatible with a celibate commitment. So is behavior which is romantic by design. I *need* to be aware of the intent of my behavior, or I'll be engaging in romantic behavior and won't even be aware of it. Then I'll be sending mixed messages about my seriousness in pursuing my commitment to a celibate life.

There are limits to the personal meaning one's intention can give to activities concerning touch, clothing and language, because of their cultural meanings. The more intimate the relationship two or more people have—that is, the more they have allowed the other or others to understand them—and the more private the expression of that intimacy, the more fully they can give their own meaning to even touch, clothing and language. But they can never completely escape the inherent cultural meanings.

I have grown tired of trying to think out what I have come to believe about relationships with people beyond my community. I fear what I have written is fragmentary and theoretical. I know I am grateful that on a Sunday evening many years ago I found the courage to climb the front porch steps of the Parker home. I am grateful that at the time I lived with brothers to whom I could confide what I had decided to do and what it meant. I am convinced, though I can't prove it even to myself, that the reason I have satisfying and intimate relationships among my brothers and with people beyond my community is that they and I have told ourselves that such relationships are possible, and have consistently chosen behaviors which allowed intimacy to arise among us.

My big treat on the occasion of my 25th anniversary of entering the novitiate was to go on vacation with Don and Mary, who were celebrating 25 years of marriage. We talked about and planned this vacation for a year. At first it was to be a vacation for just the three of us. But they conceded that since they had each other I could bring along one of my brothers in the community, and who better than their son who is also a Capuchin. In the course of the two weeks, Paul and Jerry spent a couple of days with us as well.

The days at the lake in Northern Wisconsin were filled with floating on rubber mattresses, going off individually to walk, read or just think, cooking our meals, playing cards, watching a little TV, swimming and a daily trip around the lake on the pontoon boat before supper. On the actual day of their anniversary Kevin and I cooked a champagne brunch for Don and Mary. It was a most ordinary and uneventful time for us all, and therefore exactly what we had hoped for.

After two weeks of leisure the day of our departure dawned misty and rainy. The weather did not improve as we vacuumed the cottage, gathered the laundry, did the dishes, took the garbage to the dump and packed our cars for departure.

We locked the cottage door and returned the key to the caretaker whose home is just across the way, and we stood beside our cars to say goodbye. They had as difficult a time saying "thank you" and "goodbye" as I did, I guess, because none of us got said all that was in our hearts. "Thank you and goodbye" was all we managed. I waved them off as they drove down the double-rutted road which led through the woods back to civilization. Then I got into my car and followed a few minutes later. My chest ached with the emotion I felt there as I turned my car onto the county highway, heading for another wilderness cabin for a week's retreat.

After a few minutes driving I said out loud, "Let me tell the goodness of God." I let my mind go back over the impressions left by the previous two weeks. I knew I didn't want to tell anyone in particular about the goodness of God; I just wanted to rehearse it for myself. By the time I arrived at the cabin I had decided that I would do just that and nothing more for the week. That night, by the light of a kerosene lamp, I wrote in my greenbook all those things for which I couldn't find words as I parted from Don and Mary and Kevin. When I finished, I decided that on the following day I would begin my retreat by recalling the people who had become my friends throughout my life.

I woke up early the next morning, and after breakfast I took my greenbook outside to the small patio and I sat in the sun. I began with my childhood and recalled all those I could remember who had befriended me and whom I had befriended. I wrote about them all. By evening I had filled many pages with writing and I had broken the silence of the woods with many expressions of gratitude to God for those who had been friends throughout my life. And I told the goodness of God which I had experienced through the friends I had been given.

After supper I returned to the patio to wait for dusk, and I read all I had written. I realized that God had made me through the friends he had given me. I am the person I am today largely because of the relationships I have had. And I concluded that if you can judge a man by his friends, I must be quite a man!

The next day I began the morning by reading the scriptures for the Eucharist that day. One phrase caught my attention, "God decided that I was fit to be trusted with the Good News." For some reason that directed my attention to those in my life who had been my teachers, those especially who had taught me ways of living which led me to my celibate commitment and which helped me live that commitment with meaning for myself and for others. As I sat at the small table and enjoyed the last can of Mary's homemade vegetable soup and some bread and cheese, it felt to me as though I were eating friendship. As surely as my life was to be sustained by the soup my friend had made, so my life was sustained by the friendship I experienced with Don and Mary and all the others.

God made me—through my friends, largely—and he

decided I was fit to be entrusted with the Good News. I learned that during the first two days of my retreat. The following morning I would learn something else I needed to know if I hoped to live out my days committed to a celibate life.

Chapter 11
Belonging Uniquely to God

I know that nothing I have written about the practical living out of a celibate life in response to the mystery of God's call and nothing I have written about sexuality is more important than what I want to say in this short chapter. Even though it is my most constant thought about celibacy and the most frequent entry on the subject in my greenbook, I always say it in the same way: Living a committed celibate life does not make sense and it cannot be sustained by anyone who does not regularly take the time to make himself or herself available to God in order to be touched and moved by God's Spirit. Prayer is essential to the living of a celibate life.

In what I have written so far I have tantalized my mind with ideas about sexuality and celibacy, and I have tried to find words to articulate them. Concern with the importance of praying does not seem to provide much for my mind to wrap itself around. I can't explain my abiding conviction about the absolute necessity of regular and prolonged praying; nor can I rationalize away my neglect of praying in favor of the other projects and pursuits of my life. My having spent an entire day and evening on rewriting and typing the previous chapter and having taken no time for praying causes me anxiety. It is not the anxiety of impending disaster because I have neglected what I know is essential to my life; it is the anxiety of having lived in ways other than those which I profess. I know in my heart that a committed celibate life cannot be sustained without regular and prolonged prayer because the relational void of not knowing experientially that I belong to somebody will erode even my most dogged efforts at fidelity.

Return with me for a few minutes to the wilderness cabin. On the evening of the second day of my retreat, after I had washed the dishes and lit the kerosene lamps, I turned my attention to what I should consider the next day. Nothing came to mind. After some time of rummaging around unsuccessfully for possibilities, I gave up and said to myself, "Never mind; God will provide."

When I awoke the next morning I realized that the words I had used the previous night were words Abraham had used to still his son's questioning about what sacrifice they would offer on the mountain. I decided to spend my day on the patio with Abraham, reflecting on those sections of the Book of Genesis which were about him.

I read each story—Abram's call to leave his homeland, the initial promise he received from God, his journeys, the covenant, the birth of his first son and the eventual birth of Isaac, the dismissal of Hagar and her son—and then sat with whatever reflections those passages engendered. Then I prayed whatever sentiments I found within me and I wrote it all in my greenbook as I sat in the sun on the patio.

I can see no logic to what became so clear to me by mid-afternoon. But it has remained as a guiding force in my life: God made me; he decided I was fit to be entrusted with the Good News; and now and then he wants me to himself. Nothing was written in my greenbook for the remainder of that day and very little for the following three days. Moved by the words Hagar had spoken when, during her flight from the ill treatment of Sarai, she had met God: "Surely this is the place where I, in my turn, have seen the one who sees me." I remained alone and quiet in that cabin for three days because I knew God wanted me to himself.

My friends are important because they have formed me and they sustain and support me in my celibate life. The ministry which I have been given is also important, and it helps me know I belong uniquely to God. Most of my life is spent in the company of friends or in the exercise of the gifts I've been given in ministry. But my celibate life needs something more. It requires that I allow God to have me from time to time to himself.

My two greatest temptations which take me away from praying are the chance to be with friends and my compulsion to work on some project—like completing a manuscript. And so I need to remember: God made me; he decided I was fit to be entrusted with the Good News; and now and then he wants me to himself because I am his.

In my praying I find I do with God what I do with other people in forming and nurturing intimate relationships. I disclose myself in the hearing of Another with whom I feel safe and related. I come to know I am known by God, not just because God is all-knowing, but because I have freely made myself known. In prayer God reveals himself to me, not just because I think about what I have come to know about him, but through a contemplative understanding of what those things mean to me and for me. My self-disclosure in the presence of the one who already knows me through and through, leads me to a self-awareness which is deeper still, and which I can disclose with increasing confidence. The cumulative effect of this kind of praying is an abiding and increasing realization that I belong uniquely to God.

Most people who have left a celibate commitment in order to pursue a romantic relationship have done so saying to themselves and to anyone else who would listen, "I need such a relationship. Having entered into such a relationship I can see how much I needed it all along. I'm experiencing a new joy in life, a new surge of life. I'm unfolding in freedom and spontaneity like I never knew I could."

It seems to me that such a relationship fills a void for them. And today it seems to me that the void was allowed to develop because the sense of belonging uniquely to God was not nourished. Today it appears to me that I need to develop more my own sense of belonging uniquely to God, because I too have a need to belong to somebody.

I belong uniquely to God no more than anyone else. But in order to respond to a celibate call, I need to develop intensely my own personal realization and appreciation of what is true of all of us. And I haven't taken much time for that lately.

As in most things required of celibate people, the cultivating of the sense of belonging uniquely to God is not something that only they can develop. It is within the reach of all of us. But celibate people need to develop it if they are not to suffer the void of not belonging to somebody.

The development of a celibate person's belonging uniquely to God is a gradual and life-long process. If it is not developed for some considerable period of time because of lack of praying it cannot simply be taken up again and enjoyed as if it had been constant all along. Periods of intense praying can reinitiate the sense of unique belonging, but the intensity of the new beginning should not be confused with what is experienced by those who have been constantly nurturing their relationship with God. For the constant, the experience may not be intense, but it is sustaining. New beginnings, especially if undertaken in non-crisis periods, can be trusted and accepted as invitations from God, and they can lead to the re-establishment of the relationship and the reinitiating of the sense of belonging uniquely to God.

If the re-establishment of contact, so to speak, and the reinitiation of the prayerful relationship is undertaken at the time of a relational crisis in a celibate person's life, it will possibly be done in a deliberate attempt to quickly fill in the void another relationship seems to be filling. In effect, we can reinitiate the relationship to God deliberately to compete with a romantic relationship in the hope that God will win. That's risky at best. While both can fill the same relational void, they are so distinct that they cannot be pitted against each other. Both the relationship with God in prayer and the relationship with another person in romantic pursuits may develop alongside one another. A very religious wedding is the predictable outcome.

The sense of belonging uniquely to God is not incompatible with a romantic relationship. The only incompatibility is that of pursuing a romantic relationship when we are already committed to a celibate life. If a celibate man or woman develops the sense of belonging uniquely to God in an ongoing, non-crucial way they are less likely to experience a relational void. If there is no void, the necessity for pursuing a romantic relationship will not be there. If that necessity is not present, the romantic pursuit will be less likely to begin. But once begun and if pursued, the romantic relationship will grow right along with the relationship with God.

These reflections are engendered because of the frequency with which I have heard people who are struggling with a vocational decision say that there is nothing to worry about because they are praying and their relationship to God has never been better. "Fear not for my seriousness about being open to continuing to live a celibate life," they say in effect; "I am in constant contact with God about the matter."

I have never doubted God's abiding love for me or for anyone else; God has accepted me in my moments of foolishness and self-deception as well as in my moments of fidelity and clear thinking. The sense of being close to God can develop right along with the continuing pursuit of a romantic relationship, and the eventually espoused person will be recognized as God's choicest gift to the man or woman who was formerly committed to a celibate life.

God is not a competitor with other human beings for my affection and love. God invites me to be his ally and partner in loving other human beings. He asks each person to love each other person in ways which are appropriate to the lover and the loved one. Friends, lovers, spouses are indeed God's gifts. So is a celibate relationship a gift to God and other people. Undertaking a celibate life and failing to develop its possibilities can create a relational void. Once the void is created, and a romantic relationship is pursued, the void is being filled. As long as the romantic relationship is pursued, no matter how much the relationship with God is also pursued, the predictable outcome will be something other than a celibate life both in relationship to God and to other people.

One morning I looked into the mirror as I was getting ready to face the day. As I stood there I knew somehow that for a celibate person in ministry the sense of belonging uniquely to God must include using God's gifts in doing the works. My own sense of having something to offer in workshops, or in listening to and responding to people, even my unique contribution to my province and the church, are ways in which I experience belonging uniquely to God. What is required of me in order to have my "work" or ministry contribute to that very personal sense of belonging uniquely to God is that I accept as gifts from God, and not as personal achievements, the abilities and resources I use in doing the work or the ministry.

In a recent celebration of the Sacrament of Reconciliation, I confessed an arrogance of mind which led me to put people down internally and which sometimes found externalization in my words and behavior. This arrogance is directly opposed to the development of a sense of belonging uniquely to God, because it distorts my recognition that my abilities and resources are in fact God's gifts. Instead I see them as my own accomplishments and begrudge other people imposing on the time or energy or abilities I consider my own.

An arrogant appraisal of my talents combined with the

sense that I belong to no one brings on a relational void and poses a great threat to my commitment to celibacy. It is a threat which can be countered only with regular entry into the deeper regions of personal praying. The invitation to such praying is not always pleasant. The prospect of what I will discover is sometimes frightening. But praying is an essential component of a celibate life. And it is in the regions of prayer that we celibate people belong.

I wrote in my greenbook recently something which may give a glimpse of what I experience of the kind of praying I'm trying to describe:

Alone, awake, naked, a little lonely, in the middle of the night—it has all the ingredients of an invitation from God to enter deeply into myself to find him at the quiet center of those things which seem to clamor for recognition by others, their companionship and a sense of achievement. The cold weather doesn't permit the expansiveness of being outside under the sky. The invitation is inward.

On the journey inward I fear for my very existence; a simple cold germ has wrought discomforts which raise the spector of my total disintegration. There is a large dose of purposelessness. I wonder about the meaning and worth of the enterprises in which I've spent my energies and grown tired. There's a recognition—less surprising these days—of a need which drives me to spend my energy in the hope that I will gain recognition, companionship and a sense of achievement. But, honestly, that neediness has less influence now than it used to have. And I'm glad and grateful for that. I find a sense of helplessness in doing for others what I wish I could do. But that too is not as surprising or disappointing as it used to be.

The distractions which would hold me from this inward journey have less power over my imagination. I could work on a manuscript or the retreat I must give, or even organizing tomorrow's activities. I could listen to Beethoven or enjoy my new tennis shoes on bare feet for a walk outside. I could fantasize about those others who could relieve the loneliness; I could call Paul. But all those preoccupations fail to grasp me. Having prayed for some of those I love—those who came to mind—I can lay aside even my anxious care for them and my compulsive searching for the names of others for whom I ought to pray. I bring them all, instead, to this helpless, fearful, needy, confused and failure-ridden quiet where my God awaits me. Resolutions made as recently as this morning have been broken.

My own experience of neediness is with me. It is not oppressive or surprising. It's just with me. It seems so deep that looking to any human or material source for fulfillment appears immediately futile and is easy to reject. Being with and in God as he is in me seems the only source from which I could ever find fulfillment, and from him I do not expect the satisfaction which human and material sources provide. Satisfaction is fulfillment no more than pleasure is happiness. So, I sit naked and alone, neither in pain nor looking for gratification. I just sit devoid of relieving realizations. I think it is faith which holds me here. And for that I am also grateful.

I do not approach this meeting place with hesitance as I once did, nor with deliberate step. I plunge into it because it is home, familiar now though seldom visited. I'm home. I belong here, because here lives the God to whom I belong and who already knows me and loves me in my helplessness and fear, in my neediness and confusion. Only he is less surprised than I at my failure. I used to come here with much more shame; that was before I knew this was my home. I thought I belonged out there where I looked strong and wise, where I gave to others and faced courageously those things which made others cower. I tried to make my place out there; I convinced many people that it's there I reside. But alone, awake, naked and a little lonely in the middle of the night, I feel like I'm being called home.